MEDIAEVAL SOURCES
IN TRANSLATION

33

TWO GREEK ARISTOTELIAN COMMENTATORS ON THE INTELLECT

The *De Intellectu* Attributed to
Alexander of Aphrodisias
and
Themistius' Paraphrase of Aristotle
De Anima 3.4-8

Introduction, Translation, Commentary and Notes

by

FREDERIC M. SCHROEDER
ROBERT B. TODD

PONTIFICAL INSTITUTE
OF MEDIAEVAL STUDIES

Acknowledgment

This book has been published with the help of a grant from the Canadian Federation for the Humanities using funds provided by the Social Sciences and Humanities Research Council of Canada.

CANADIAN CATALOGUING IN PUBLICATION DATA

Main entry under title:

Two Greek Aristotelian commentators on the intellect

(Mediaeval sources in translation, ISSN 0316-0874 ; 33)
Includes bibliographical references.
ISBN 0-88844-283-1

1. Aristotle. De anima. 2. Intellect — Early works to 1800. I. Schroeder, Frederic Maxwell, 1937- . II. Todd, Robert B. III. Pontifical Institute of Mediaeval Studies. IV. Alexander, of Aphrodisias. De intellectu. V. Themistius. Paraphrase of Aristotle De anima 3.4. VI. Series.

B535.A63D4 1990   128'.3   C89-094454-7

PRINTED BY UNIVERSA, WETTEREN, BELGIUM

Contents

INTRODUCTION

THE *DE INTELLECTU*

THEMISTIUS: PARAPHRASE OF *DE ANIMA* 3.4-8

To the memory of our fathers
W.F. Schroeder and H.B. Todd

In the later Middle Ages, that is after the adoption of Aristotelianism, all the science men had was expressed in the Aristotelian terminology of form and matter, and for this reason the relation between soul and body did not seem unique or even very puzzling. If Aristotle and St. Thomas were right, the body's possession of a soul was only a special case of a relationship of which examples could be found everywhere in nature. It was true that there had been a lot of obscure discussion about the difficulty of accounting for the active intellect ...

W. Kneale, *On Having a Mind*
(Eddington Memorial Lecture, Cambridge: 1962), p. 23.

Preface

Chapter 5 in the third book of Aristotle's *De Anima*, the famous discussion of the so-called active intellect, occupies only sixteen lines in the standard Oxford text, but the ratio between this passage and the exegesis that it has received since antiquity is undoubtedly higher than for any other Aristotelian text, and perhaps for any single text in the history of philosophy. Although many aspects of this remarkable venture in philosophical scholarship have been studied, much relevant source material has yet to be translated into modern languages and closely examined. The present work contains translations and analyses of commentaries on *De Anima* 3.5 and its surrounding context made by Greek Aristotelian writers in late antiquity. The first is an opusculum, the *De Intellectu*, traditionally attributed to Aristotle's major ancient commentator Alexander of Aphrodisias (fl. ca. AD 200), the second a portion of a paraphrase of the *De Anima* by the fourth century commentator Themistius. Both texts were subsequently translated into Arabic and Latin. They played an important role in the philosophical and theological debates of the thirteenth century, and continued to be studied by Aristotelians of the Renaissance. They are also available in modern editions that could serve as a reliable basis for our translations. By presenting these works primarily as documents of Greek Aristotelianism we hope to foster a fuller appreciation of texts that are in many ways as challenging as that brief and obscure chapter of the *De Anima* from which they take their inspiration. We hope that this will contribute to the revival of interest in the Greek Aristotelian commentators evident in recent years.

There is of course an enormous body of surviving exegetical literature on the Aristotelian noetic surviving from later antiquity. It includes, for example, the treatise *De Anima* by Alexander of

Aphrodisias (see Introduction pp. 6-22), and commentaries on
Aristotle's *De Anima* by Simplicius, Philoponus and Stephanus of
Alexandria. But of this material only the two texts presented here,
along with Philoponus' commentary on *De Anima* 3.4-8, were
available in Latin translations in the later middle ages. We have
not included Philoponus' work since it is available to medievalists
in a modern edition by Verbeke (1966); also an English translation by W. Charlton will appear shortly in the series *The Ancient
Commentators on Aristotle*. Philoponus' exegesis, in any case,
belongs to the Neoplatonic period of ancient Aristotelianism. By
contrast, the *De Intellectu* and Themistius' paraphrase offer a
more direct approach to Aristotelian thought, and can be legiti-
mately characterized as specimens of Peripatetic exegesis. It
therefore makes philosophical as well as historical sense to
present these two texts separately.

We have chosen to structure our discussions of the two texts
differently. A growing interest in Alexander of Aphrodisias in
recent years has made the *De Intellectu* an important piece of
evidence in debates about Alexander's background and the
evolution of his noetic. At the same time its very authenticity has
been challenged. Accordingly, the first part of the Introduction
has had to deal with some controversial issues. Themistius'
paraphrase, by contrast, has been rather neglected, particularly by
students of ancient philosophy, and so the second part of the
Introduction could only be a basic survey of an area in which
much work remains to be done.

Our commentaries also differ in a way that reflects the different
character of the texts. The *De Intellectu* is an epitome that
proceeds at some distance from the relevant Aristotelian texts.
The commentary required by this material had, therefore, to be
cast in a more discursive form. Themistius, on the other hand,
generally follows the Aristotelian text closely. Commentary on
such material seemed best presented in the form of notes to the
translation.

Decisions regarding the translation of important terminology
are indicated in the Glossary; we refer in particular to the list of

equivalents that we have adopted for the various epithets of the intellect. We also discuss problems of translation in the course of our commentaries. One particularly difficult decision worth noting here has involved two semantically related triads central to the Aristotelian noetic that retain their affinity in the traditional Latin versions: viz. *nous/ noein/ noêton* (*intellectus/intellegere/ intelligibile*) and *aisthêsis/aisthanestai/ aisthêton* (*sensus/ sentire/ sensibile*). Like many modern translators we have not chosen to anglicize the Latin and so have severed the elements of the first of these triads by using *intellect/ think/ object of thought*, while for the second employing *perception/ perceive/ object of perception*. Also the introduction of the term "object" presents the greatest risk of confusion in suggesting a misleading dichotomy between the activity and that with which it is identical in Aristotelian doctrine. But the reader will be forewarned.

Frederic M. Schroeder had responsibility for the parts of this work involving the *De Intellectu*, Robert B. Todd for those involving Themistius' paraphrase. Each, however, examined and criticized the other's work; separate authorial reponsibility does not, therefore, preclude acknowledgment that the final product is the result of close collaboration. Both authors also acknowledge the helpful criticism of readers for the Pontifical Institute of Mediaeval Studies and the Canadian Federation for the Humanities.

We have tried to take account of the secondary literature available prior to completing our revision of the manuscript in mid-1988. R.W. Sharples' essay on Alexander, published in *Aufstieg und Niedergang der römischen Welt* 2.36.2 in 1987 and H.B. Gottschalk's discussion in the same volume (1987) reached us during this process. Some references to Sharples' review of the scholarly literature on Alexander of Aphrodisias have been included in the discussion of the *De Intellectu*, though it was not possible to take full account of his important contribution. Gottschalk's survey of Aristotelian philosophy in the two centuries before Alexander includes a valauble discussion of Alexander's teachers and so has bearing on the first part of the Intro-

duction. We have also been unable to include references to
discussions of the influence of the two texts studied here in some
contributions to the recently published *Cambridge History of
Renaissance Philosophy* ed. Quentin Skinner and the late Charles
B. Schmitt (Cambridge: 1988).

F.M.S.

July 1988   R.B.T.

Abbreviations and Conventions

In the translations [ ] signifies a supplement added for explanation or clarification; it is used more selectively for words that are obviously to be understood (see the Glossary). < >, apart from its use in headings, signifies a conjectural supplement to the Greek text. ( ) is used as a normal device of punctuation.

The Bibliography provides entries for all references to major primary sources, and to secondary sources cited by the author's name or, in the case of multiple entries, by name and year of publication. The following abbreviations should be noted:

CAG	*Commentaria in Aristotelem Graeca.* The Greek Aristotelian commentators will be referred to by the title, and volume page and line number of the standard modern edition, Berlin: 1883-1907; this information is abbreviated for works fully cited in Part A of the Bibliography.
Diels-Kranz	H. Diels and W. Kranz, *Die Fragmente der Vorsokratiker.* 6th. ed. (Berlin: 1952).
LSJ	H. Liddell, R. Scott, H.S. Jones, *A Greek-English Lexicon,* 9th. ed. (Oxford: 1940).
Plotinus	Cited from *Plotini Opera,* ed. P. Henry and H.-R. Schwyzer, editio minor, Oxford Classical Texts, 3 vols. Oxford: 1964-1982.
SA	*Supplementum Aristotelicum*; see Part A of the Bibliography under Alexander of Aphrodisias.
SVF	*Stoicorum Veterum Fragmenta,* ed. H. Von Arnim, vols. 1-3 (Leipzig: 1903-1905); vol. 4 (Indices), ed. M. Adler (Leipzig: 1924).

INTRODUCTION

1. THE *DE INTELLECTU* ATTRIBUTED TO ALEXANDER OF APHRODISIAS

Historical Importance of the De Intellectu

The *De Intellectu,* commonly attributed to Alexander of Aphrodisias, the acknowledged dean of later Greek commentators on Aristotle, has attracted the attention of scholars in the fields of Arabic and Jewish theology and philosophy, the theology and philosophy of the Latin middle ages and the intellectual history of the Renaissance. This work has also received the attention of classicists specializing in the philosophy of late antiquity. There is, however, no adequate translation with introduction and commentary, written from this perspective, that presents a scholarly treatment of the work especially for those in other areas who are interested in it. It is with these reasons in mind that this study is offered.[1]

Porphyry informs us that Alexander of Aphrodisias was among the authorities read in the seminar of Plotinus.[2] There is no conclusive argument, however, that the *De Intellectu* was among

---

[1] The text of the *De Intellectu* on which our translation is based is that of I. Bruns, *De Anima Liber cum Mantissa,* SA 2.1 (Berlin: 1887) 106.18-113.24. The appendix in Finnegan (1956a) 200-202 was consulted for the witness of the Arabic versions and Théry 74-82 for the evidence of the medieval Latin version. Fotinis' translation with commentary on the *De Anima* of Alexander of Aphrodisias and the *De Intellectu* has not been well received by Donini (1982) 247 and note 50 who is critical of the scholarship in Fotinis' commentary, accusing him of inexcusable errors and of ignoring the contemporary literature. Preus is more generous and finds the translation "generally reliable and clear" (427), although he is critical (428) of Fotinis' habit of supplying words gratuitously and also of his occasional omissions.

[2] Porphyry *Vita Plotini* 14.13.

the works consulted by Plotinus and his students.[3] As we shall
see, it is not clear, in any case, that Alexander is the author of the
De Intellectu. There is also no evidence that the *De Intellectu* was
known in later antiquity and the earliest Greek manuscript is from
the tenth century.[4]

In Baghdad, in the ninth century, the *De Intellectu* was translated into Arabic in the school of Ḥunain ibn Isḥāq (which
included his son Isḥāq ibn Ḥunain).[5] It has been argued that (in
this translation) the *De Intellectu* exerted a major influence upon
the thought of al-Kindi, al-Fārābī, Ibn Sīnā and Ibn Rushd.[6]

---

[3] Schwyzer cols. 573-574 finds only three parallels between Alexander and
Plotinus which would compel us to recognize the relationship of source
(Plotinus 4.3 [27].20.15-16 and Alexander *Mantissa* 115.32-33; Plotinus 2.7
[37].1.53-54 and Alexander *De Mixtione* 220.14-15; Plotinus 4.7 [2].6.11-14
and Alexander *De Anima* 68.8-13). Some of the literature would suggest that
there is a considerable degree of influence upon Plotinus (see Armstrong;
Henry; Rist (1962); Merlan (1963) 39-40; 47-52; 77-83; Hager). Rist (1966a),
with special reference to Hager, adopts a conservative position. Linguistic
parallels do not of themselves compel us to recognize a relationship of source.
The possibility of influence from sources lost to us must also be considered.
Blumenthal (1968) casts doubt even upon one of Schwyzer's identifications
(Plotinus 4.3 [27].20.15-16 and Alexander *De Anima* 115.32-33), although he
accepts Henry's addition to Schwyzer's list (Plotinus 4.7 [2].6 and Alexander
De Anima 61-63). Donini (1974) 19-23 sees Plotinus making use both of
Alexander *De Anima* and the *De Intellectu,* but see Schroeder (1984) 241-242.
Slezák 135-143 discusses the influence of Alexander on Plotinus and introduces
some new parallels, including passages from the *De Intellectu.* Discouraged,
however, by Rist's reply to Hager, he allows for the possibility that these
apparent parallels might be misleading. Schroeder (1984) reviews this discussion and sees in Plotinus 4.5 [29].7.33-49 polemic against Alexander *De Anima*
42.19-43.11. Becchi 90 argues that the reference to Alexander in Porphyry *Vita
Plotini* 14 is not to Alexander of Aphrodisias, but to Alexander of Aegae. For
the relationship between Alexander of Aphrodisias and Plotinus, see now
Sharples (1987) 1220-1223.

[4] Moraux (1942) 207-221 discovers apparent references to the *De Intellectu*
in Philoponus (sixth century); cf. Verbeke (1966) 13-14. None of these is
compelling.

[5] There is some confusion whether the translation was executed by Ḥunain
ibn Isḥāq or his son (Théry 20-21; Badawi [1968] 97). For the view that the
translation proceeds from the school of Ḥunain ibn Isḥāq, which included his
son, see Peters (1968a) 60.

[6] Théry 18-21; Peters (1968a) 59-61; Cranz (1961) 80.

However, there is some doubt that this treatise was a source for al-Kindi and al-Fārābī (who each wrote a treatise bearing the title *De Intellectu* known to the medieval Latin West).[7]

The *De Intellectu* was available in Latin translation from the end of the twelfth century. A partial version, attributed to Gerard of Cremona, which drew upon both Arabic and Greek sources, has been preserved intact.[8] For the student of the Latin middle ages, the fortune of the *De Intellectu* is associated with the papal decrees of the thirteenth century, which forbade the teaching of all but the logical works of Aristotle in the University of Paris. The alleged materialism of its psychology and its implication of human mortality would be repugnant to Catholic teaching. Apart from any independent influence, it was significant for its association with Ibn Rushd (Averroes) whose doctrine of monopsychism (not to be found in the *De Intellectu*) was to be condemned, especially for its implication that the human individual is mortal.[9]

The Arabic version of the *De Intellectu*, which proceeded from the school of Ḥunain ibn Isḥāq, was translated into Hebrew in the fourteenth century by Samuel ben Juda ben Meschullam. The Jews did not develop a school of Peripatetic translation as did the Arabs and the scholars of the Latin West. The Spanish Jews did, however, have direct access to Arabic translations. The Alexandrian noetic (and possibly the *De Intellectu*) thereby exerted an influence on Jewish thought.[10]

[7] Finnegan (1957); Finnegan (1956-2) discovers in Ibn Sīnā's refutation of the "Porphyrians" a reference to the *De Intellectu*. This is accepted by Davidson 169-170. The influence of this treatise upon Ibn Rushd is not in dispute. For the treatises entitled *De Intellectu* by al-Kindi and al-Fārābī, see Gilson 27-38; 115 note 1; Massignon 151-158.

[8] For the common attribution of this work to Gerard of Cremona, see Théry 74, 82. This is called into doubt by Cranz (1961) 111. Cranz (1961) and (1971) offers a detailed catalogue of the medieval and renaissance translations of the *De Intellectu*.

[9] See Théry; Van Steenberghen (1955) and (1970); Cranz (1961) 80; for the influence of the *De Intellectu* on the noetic of the medieval Latin West generally, see Grabmann (1929) and (1936) and Wilpert.

[10] Günsz 35-37; on the influence of the Alexandrian noetic on Maimonides, see Günsz 27-32.

The school of Padua in the fifteenth and sixteenth centuries inherited and developed philosophical directions, especially Averroism, which had begun in Paris in the thirteenth century.[11] In the Italy of the Renaissance, the *De Intellectu* was translated from Greek into Latin,[12] and the *De Intellectu* influenced such figures as Nicoletto Vernia and Agostino Nifo.[13]

Biography and Significance of Alexander of Aphrodisias

We know little of the life of Alexander of Aphrodisias. We do know that Herminus and Sosigenes were his teachers.[14] Alexander dedicates the *De Fato* to Septimius Severus and Caracalla (164.3). This seems to indicate that the work was written between 198 and 209 AD.[15] It is possible that Alexander had been appointed to the chair of Aristotelian philosophy established by Marcus Aurelius in 176 AD.[16] It is not even clear that the

---

[11] See Randall (1961) 20-21.

[12] The Latin version of Girolamo Bagolino was published in Verona in 1516; Angelo Canini's Latin translation of the *De Anima Mantissa* (which contains the *De Intellectu)* was published in Venice in 1546. The *editio princeps* of Alexander's *De Anima* and the *De Anima Mantissa* was published in Venice in 1534. See Cranz (1961) 81; Movia (1970b) 17.

[13] Mahoney (1969). For recent bibliography on the influence of Alexander of Aphrodisias, see Sharples (1987) 1223-1224.

[14] For Herminus see Simplicius *In De Caelo* (CAG 7) 430.32ff.; for Sosigenes see Alexander *In Meteorologica* (CAG 3.2) 143.13. The latter is, of course, to be distinguished from the astronomer, cf. Th. Martin. The question of Aristotle of Mytilene will be discussed below pp. 22-33.

[15] Todd (1976) 1 and note 3 questions the traditional lower terminus of 211 on the grounds that Alexander would not have failed to mention Geta who was created Augustus in 209. Moraux (1981) 641 accepts Todd's chronology; Bastait's' chronology also agrees with Todd. However, Montanari 1438-1439 challenges Todd: the manuscript authority for the works of Alexander, he believes, derives almost certainly (*secondo ogni verisimiglianza,* 1438) from the School of Athens (although see note 16 below). The Athenian editors would, especially in the case of an official dedication, have observed the *damnatio memoriae* of Geta.

[16] Dio Cassius 72.31; Philostratus *Vitae Sophistarum* 566; Lucian *Eunuchus* 3.7-11 and Todd (1976) 1 note 2; 6 note 29. Lynch 193 states, on the basis of the dedication of the *De Fato,* that Alexander worked at Rome. Lynch

Aphrodisias is the familiar site in Caria, although the rich culture of that city renders this probable.[17]

Alexander was the first of the commentators for whom we have an extensive number of commentaries. Along with Themistius he represents a relatively orthodox form of exegesis that was capable of making a reading of Aristotle without reference to Neoplatonism.[18] He was known to the subsequent Greek tradition as the commentator *par excellence*.[19] His reputation loomed large among the Arabic philosophers, the thinkers of the medieval Latin West and the School of Padua.[20]

214, however, is more cautious. He argues that Alexander may have been appointed to an imperial chair in Rome or Alexandria. Such chairs were not necessarily occupied by scholarchs, but the appointment could be assigned to "an itinerant teacher or a distinguished philosopher or scientist." In the first century AD Vespasian established such a chair in Rome (Philostratus *Vitae Sophistarum* 580; 589; 627; cf. Suetonius *Vespasian* 18) and Antoninus Pius had established municipal chairs in other cities (*Historia Augusta*, Capitolinus, *Life of Antoninus Pius* 11.3). Moraux (1973) 523 relics on Lynch 193 and argues that there is no compelling evidence in the dedication of the *De Fato* for Alexander's tenure at Rome. Donini (1982) 220 and 245 note 26 follows Moraux in this. Thillet (1984) xxxvi-li reviews both Greek and Arabic evidence for the relationship between Alexander and Galen. It appears that Galen *De anatomicis administrationibus* 2.218.6 Kühn conflates Alexander of Aphrodisias with Alexander of Damascus. The latter is depicted as holding the chair of Aristotelianism in Athens. Thillet argues that this is really a reference to Alexander of Aphrodisias. On the hypothesis that this information is provided by way of revision in Galen's old age, Thillet argues that the chair in question would be that established by Marcus Aurelius in 176 AD. Galen would be here confusing Alexander of Damascus, who had held a municipal chair of Aristotelianism in Athens and who had studied with Galen, with Alexander of Aphrodisias who, at the time of Galen's revision, currently held the imperial chair of this subject. Thillet also provides, on the basis of Arabic evidence, an argument for the possibility that Alexander and Galen knew each other in Rome.

[17] Robert and Todd (1976) 1 note 4.

[18] Sharples (1983) 15.

[19] Simplicius *In Physica* (CAG 10) 1170.13; 1176.32; Olympiodorus *In Meteorologica* (CAG 12.2) 263.19-21 and Sharples (1983) 15 note 92; for further references see now Sharples (1987) note 23.

[20] Théry 18-27; 34-67; Hamelin; Cranz (1961) 80; Badawi (1968) 94-99; Pines (1961); Davidson; Brown. On the School of Padua, see Cranz (1961) 81; Randall; Mahoney (1969).

The Authorship of the De Intellectu

Three significant psychological treatises are attributed to Alexander of Aphrodisias. We know of the existence of a lost commentary on the *De Anima* of Aristotle from references in the ancient commentators.[21] Alexander's *De Anima,* which is not a commentary but a personal treatise on the soul,[22] survives and is certainly authentic.[23] We also possess the *De Intellectu,* which is preserved in a diverse collection of psychological writings known as the *Mantissa,* a disparaging title conferred upon it by the editor Bruns.[24]

The *De Intellectu* was regarded as a sort of second *De Anima* until its authenticity as a work of Alexander of Aphrodisias was called into question in 1942 by Moraux, who detected such a divergence of doctrine between the two treatises that he concluded that they could not both be by the same author, even if we made allowance for intellectual development. Since we know the *De Anima* to belong to Alexander, we should therefore, he argued, reject the Alexandrian authorship of the *De Intellectu.*

In both works the human intellect is tripartite, consisting of (1) a potential or material intellect, (2) an intellect in a state of possession (the *habitus* of the medieval translations) and (3) an intellect in actuality. Moraux argued that they differed radically in their account of the function of these phases of intellect. In the *De Anima* the potential or material intellect is a complete faculty, capable of abstracting form from matter, while in the *De Intellectu* it is merely an embryonic form of intellect that has yet to develop to this stage. Again, in the *De Anima* the intellect in a state of possession is a storehouse of forms accumulated through retention of forms abstracted from matter by the potential or material intellect. In the *De Intellectu,* on the other hand, the intellect in

---

[21] Zeller 818 note 2.

[22] Ed. I. Bruns sa 2.1:1-100.

[23] For the explicit references see Philoponus *In De Anima* (cag 15) 159.18-19; Michael of Ephesus *In Parva Naturalia* (cag 22.1) 135.24-28.

[24] At sa 2.1: 101-186 (*De Intellectu* = 106.18-113.24).

the state of possession is (like the potential or material intellect in the *De Anima*) a faculty capable of abstracting forms from matter.

In both treatises there is, apart from the human intellect, a productive intellect that is divine. The action of this intellect is (in the *De Anima*) indirect. Light, by the very act of being supremely visible, causes visibility for visible objects. On this analogy, the productive intellect, by the very fact of its being supremely an object of thought, renders the forms that are abstracted from matter by the potential or material intellect objects of thought. It thus indirectly contributes to the formation of the human intellect. In the *De Intellectu* the productive intellect imparts the intellect in the state of possession to the embryonic potential or material intellect. On the analogy of light, it is seen together with its concomitants. It is by reference to the productive intellect as primary object of intellective vision that the human intellect is able to abstract form as object of thought from matter.

At *De Anima* 2.18-22 Alexander argues that, to understand the nature of the soul, it is necessary first to examine the body that is ensouled. All bodies are either simple or composite. To understand body it is easier and preferable to begin with the simple bodies, the elements earth, air, fire and water. Every body is composed of matter and form. The form of a simple body is identical with its primary qualities. Thus the form of fire is heat and dryness and the concomitant lightness (5.4-9). The matter of fire is that which receives such a form and is capable of receiving its contraries (cold and wet). Neither the matter nor the form is fire, but their combination (5.18-6.2), although fire is what it is with reference to its form (6.21-23). Simple bodies combine to form composite bodies that display greater disparity (7.21-8.13). Form in biological bodies is soul (9.11-14; 11.2).

Alexander's doctrine that the soul arises from the fusion or composition of elements represents for Moraux a materialism remote from the true psychology of Aristotle.[25] Donini shows that

---

[25] Moraux (1942) 29; 169; 173.

Alexander, who at least by his profession is faithful to Aristotle (*De Anima* 2.4-9), remains Aristotelian in an important sense.[26] Aristotle says that the study of the soul belongs to the domain of physics because the study of the soul is necessarily the study of soul in body (1.1, 403a28). Alexander construes these words as an invitation to engage in the kind of account we have just given. Donini shows that this rests upon Alexander's study of the *De Generatione et Corruptione* and the *Meteorologica*. Of course, the philosophical distance between Alexander and his master may remain great, even if a step by step examination of his argument reveals apparently legitimate Aristotelian roots.

Moraux sees in Alexander's theory of the origin of the soul the basis and foundation of his entire psychology. The soul is far from being the cause that determines the constitution of the body, its internal structure and its entire development, as in Aristotle. On Moraux's view, it is the organization of the body that engenders the soul. The soul is the result, indeed an accident, that proceeds from a corporeal mixture. The Alexandrian noetic therefore proceeds from the general principles of Alexander's psychology. The intellect accordingly develops in a soul-body complex of greater diversity and subtlety than may be found in vegetative or other ensouled entities. Like soul itself, intellect is a result, even an accident, of such a combination. Yet in faithfulness to the text of Aristotle, Alexander endows such an intellect (which is, in the first phase of its development, described as potential or material) with the ability to abstract, conserve and know form as object of thought. It is, says Moraux: "Une non-substance qui agit: voilà bien la plus grave hérésie qui puisse sortir de la bouche d'un Aristotélicien."[27]

Donini argues correctly that a closer reading of the *De Anima* of Alexander will show that Moraux is not entirely fair to Alexander in discovering such contradictions.[28] Aristotle in *De*

---

[26] Donini (1970) 64-68; 73-74; 82; 87; 89; 94-96; 107; cf. Zorzetti; cf. also Donini (1982) 231-232.

[27] Moraux (1942) 173.

[28] Donini (1970); cf. Schroeder (1982) 117-119. Also see Sharples (1987)

Anima 1.4, 407b27-408a30, refutes arguments that assert that the soul is a harmony. Alexander in *De Anima* 24.18-26 offers a discussion of the subject that contains important differences from the Aristotelian argument. Alexander maintains (24.18-25.4) that if we assert that the soul is a form supervening upon the mixture or fusion of its component bodies, it does not follow that the soul is a harmony. While the soul may not exist apart from that mixture, it need not be identical with it. It is rather a *dunamis* that supervenes upon this fusion or mixture. It is like the *dunamis* of a drug, its power to heal, which arises from the mixture of its chemical elements in a certain proportion, yet is neither those elements nor the proportion itself. Thus we may, with Moraux, see the soul as a result of a combination of bodily elements. However, we need not regard it as it as merely an accident of that combination. As such the soul would have no true life of its own.

The word *dunamis* (usually translated as "potency") in Aristotle may have the sense of power to act, as well as power to be acted upon.[29] Now while Alexander and Aristotle both define soul as form, Alexander does not follow Aristotle *De Anima* 2.1, 412a21-28 in identifying this form with first entelechy, but with a *dunamis*. Alexander nonetheless means by the terms form and *dunamis* what Aristotle means by first entelechy.[30] In Aristotle the analogy by which first entelechy is explained is with knowledge and its application. We may have knowledge even before we apply it (e.g., even in sleep). Alexander *De Anima* 9.14-23 offers the example of earth and weight to explain the soul as a *dunamis*. The form and *dunamis* of earth is weight. The weight is perfect and

---

1181: "It also seems characteristic of Alexander's approach that he tends to consider particular points one by one, rather than being concerned to establish his own position on the whole of a topic in a systematic way. In spite of his undoubted critical acumen, he at times takes Aristotle's text in a forced way in order to support his own views ... ."

[29] *Metaphysics* 9.1, 1046a9-19.

[30] Cf. Alexander *De Anima* 9.14-23; 15.29-16.10; 80.16-24 and Donini (1970) 87 note 2 and Schroeder (1982) 118-119.

complete even in the absence of the downward motion that is its actuality and second perfection.

It is instructive in this context to observe that Galen, in what he claims is an Aristotelian argument, identifies the soul with the corporeal mixture itself.[31] He also contests an earlier view to the effect that the soul is not to be identified with the mixture itself, but rather is to be considered a *dunamis* which supervenes upon the mixture, the view we find in Alexander.[32]

Moraux discovers a fundamental contradiction in Alexander's description of the first phase of human thought as potential or material.[33] This phase is compared by Alexander *De Anima*

---

[31] *Quod animi mores corporis temperamenta sequantur,* ed. I. Müller (*Galeni Scripta Minora* vol. 2 [Leipzig: 1891]) 44.9-45.3.

[32] The possibility that Alexander may have been acquainted with this Galenic treatise is entertained by Donini (1970) 96-107 and Donini (1974) 150-156, although Donini does not allow this thesis more than a great measure of verisimilitude (Donini [1974] 151). Todd (1977) 125-128 argues that the consultation of this text by Alexander is not a necessary hypothesis. Donini (1982) 246 note 47 objects to the general tone of Todd's argument for neglecting his discussion (Donini [1974] 127-150; cf. now Donini [1982] 227-228) on Galenic themes in Alexander *De Fato.* For Arabic evidence for the dependence of Alexander on Galen see Nutton 318-322. Alexander's refusal to identify the soul with the corporeal mixture itself demonstrates at least his distance from a materialism of the kind we encounter in Galen; on this question of Alexander's dependence upon Galen, see now Sharples (1987) 1203. Donini (1971) 82-93 and Donini (1982) 231-233 argue that Alexander's views upon the arising of the soul from the fusion of corporeal elements is derived from a misinterpretation of Aristotle *De Anima* 1.4, 408a24-26; cf. Philoponus *In De Anima* (CAG 15) 151.27-152.10. Galen (in the text cited above, note 31) represents his source (Müller at 44.12 supplies Andronicus) as stating that the soul is both a mixture (of corporeal elements) and a *dunamis* which supervenes upon the mixture. Donini (1970) 102 expresses doubt with respect to the reference to Andronicus because it rests upon editorial conjecture, but (1982) 98 note 46 affirms it upon the basis of reference to the presence of the reference in the Arabic translation from the school of Ḥunain ibn Isḥāq (see Moraux [1973] 134 note 9; [1978] 285 and note 6). See, however, the discussion of Todd (1977) who, apart from this controversy, sees no compelling reason to accept the reference to Andronicus, but is willing (127) to entertain the idea "that attempts among Aristotelians to consider the relation between Aristotle's theory of the soul and his doctrine of the mixture of the elements predate Alexander." On the question of Galen's reference to Andronicus, see now Sharples (1987) 1203.

[33] Moraux (1942) 70-71; 75; 117-118; 173-174.

84.24-26 to a writing tablet or, more precisely, to the condition in a tablet of not containing writing. Moraux objects that for the first phase of intellect to advance from utter passivity to the acts of abstracting, conserving and knowing form would be as if the tablet were to cover itself with writing.[34]

Schroeder, in an article published in 1982, adapts the approaches of Donini to demonstrate that this first phase of intellection in Alexander is not potential in the sense that it is something utterly passive that must be endowed with active characteristics to bring it into harmony with the Aristotelian text. It is rather potential in Alexander's special sense of first entelechy. Complete in itself, it may advance to further perfections. Schroeder also re-examines the description of the first phase of intellection as material. The suggestion that this first phase is material might seem to denote that the material intellect is passive in the reception of forms, rather than an active faculty. It is, however, to be observed that Alexander compares (84.24-85.5) the material intellect, not simply to a writing tablet, but to the condition in a tablet of not containing writing and to the suitability for being written upon. The suitability for being written upon is not affected by the act of writing. The material intellect therefore does not serve as matter to the forms it receives.[35]

This idea may be better understood from some antecedent remarks (83.23-84.24) on perception. An unensouled object, Alexander notes, may serve as matter to the affection of heat. While an organ of perception such as the eye may serve as matter to and be affected by what is seen, the faculty of perception such as sight is not itself affected. Perception is a faculty of judgment or discernment, not merely an affection. Perception perceives perceptible forms as embedded in matter. Intellect abstracts the

---

[34] Ibid., 75.

[35] Schroeder (1982) is replying to Bazán (1973) whose argument for the authenticity of the *De Intellectu* as a work of Alexander rests upon his acceptance of the contradictions which Moraux (1942) finds in Alexander's *De Anima*. Bazán (1973) will be discussed below where we shall have occasion to review the relevance of the productive intellect to this discussion.

forms addressed by perception from their material substrate and in this act advances to thought (84.6-9). Perception is not itself changed in the act of perception, although the organ of perception is affected.

Intellect, which is without such an organ, acts to abstract forms from matter and is not itself affected by them, nor does it serve as matter to them. In the absence of an organ such as the organ of perception it enjoys a greater independence (84.10-14). Thus the description of the first phase of intellect as material, paradoxical as it may seem, does not carry with it the requirement that it be utterly passive. It may be said in summation that the contradictions Moraux discovered in 1942 with respect to the description of this phase as potential or material do not stand; indeed, Moraux himself has since softened his earlier views in these matters.[36]

It may then be asked, why does Alexander bother at all to call this phase of intellect "material?" All men have the material intellect by nature. Only the sage, through learning and habituation, advances to the possession of the acquired intellect. It is with reference to the reception of this acquired intellect that the material intellect is so called. It may receive the acquired intellect as its form and completion.[37]

Bazán agrees that the noetic of Alexander *De Anima* presents the contradictions Moraux had described in his earlier study. It may be recalled that Moraux had also argued that the *De Anima* and the *De Intellectu* so contradict each other that they may not be seen as proceeding from the hand of the same author, even if we allow for an intellectual development between them. Bazán, by contrast, has argued that the *De Intellectu* is a work of Alexander's maturity because it corrects the internal contradictions of the *De Anima*; the latter can be regarded, therefore, as an earlier work.[38]

---

[36] Moraux (1978a) 297-305.
[37] *De Anima* 81.22-82.3 and Schroeder (1982) 120-121.
[38] Bazán (1973); see Moraux (1942) 132-134.

Now at *De Intellectu* 108.16-26, Bazán argues, the productive intellect is described as form and object of thought free of any material substrate. The potential or material intellect in man addresses itself in the first instance to this form with reference to which it is then capable of abstracting enmattered form. As it is thus already actualized before its address to enmattered form, it need not present the contradiction found by Bazán that a passive entity may of itself advance to actuality, as in the *De Anima*.[39]

In 1974 Donini suggested that the *De Intellectu* is to be ascribed to Alexander's juvenalia.[40] The doctrine of the immaterial forms, transcendent objects of thought advanced in the *De Anima*, in his view, appears more sophisticated than the doctrine of the productive intellect as one form and object of thought put forth in the *De Intellectu*. The causality by which thought is engendered in the *De Intellectu* appears naive to him.

Moraux has abandoned much of his earlier position, stressing similarities between the two works, especially the tripartite structure of the intellect. He for this reason disagrees with Bazán, but finds attractive Bazán's suggestion that the *De Intellectu* should be regarded as a work of Alexander's maturity.[41]

As we have seen, in his reply to Bazán in 1982, Schroeder argues against Moraux's earlier view that the *De Anima* does not present those contradictions with respect to the potential or material intellect of which it is accused. Therefore, Schroeder contends, it is not necessary that its doctrine be corrected by the *De Intellectu* in the manner suggested by Bazán.

The *De Intellectu* reads very much like derivative material. This may be seen from a comparison with the *De Anima*. The latter presents, not only a coherent body of doctrine, but a program of argument. Alexander begins with the rise of the soul from corporeal mixture. He then describes the various types of soul that proceed from increasingly complex combinations of elements

---

[39] Cf. Bazán (1973) 478-484, especially 481-482.
[40] Donini (1974) 59-62; he is not engaged here in refuting Bazán (1973).
[41] Moraux (1978a) 269 and note 69.

until this process reaches the intellective soul in man. Man shares in common with animals a progression from sensation to imagination to memory. His specific difference is that he may proceed further to the abstraction, conservation and knowledge of enmattered form. Alexander then presents the development of intellection through three phases: the potential or material intellect; intellect in the state of possession; and the intellect in actuality, demonstrating the reason for each evolutionary advance. The *De Intellectu,* on the other hand, presents us with a terse and summary list of the three phases of intellection and their functions and thus appears derivative.

The unoriginal character of the *De Intellectu* is worth illustrating in detail. The psychological evolution of the *De Anima* of Alexander culminates in a splendid meeting of the natural and metaphysical orders of the universe.[42] This conclusion emerges from an examination of the difficult crux that occurs in Alexander's treatment of the analogy of the productive intellect to light in Aristotle *De Anima* 3.5. In this passage, Alexander says:

> In all things that which is especially and supereminently what it is is the cause for other things of being such as they are. That which is especially visible, such as light, is the cause for other things of their being visible and that which is especially and primarily good is the cause for other things of their being good. Other things are judged good by their contribution to this. That which is especially and by its own nature object of thought is, it is reasonable to maintain, the cause of the intellection of other objects of thought. Such an entity would be the productive intellect. *(De Anima* 88.26-89.6)

If we confine ourselves to the part of this statement that asserts that what is supereminently visible is the cause for other things of their visibility just as good things are rendered good by that which is supereminently good, we may seem to be in the presence of a Platonic (or proleptically even a Neoplatonic) pattern of

---

[42] Schroeder (1981).

causation, as Merlan claims.[43] The principle stated in this passage was falsely understood by Moraux to be enunciated by the scholastic formula *propter quod alia, id maximum tale*; that is, that that which causes the existence of a quality in some other thing must possess that quality in the highest degree.[44] It is rather the case that Alexander here assumes the supreme intelligibility of the productive intellect or the supreme luminosity of the source of light as a premiss of argument. Lloyd properly observes, "Alexander was not at that point trying to prove the *existence* of something supremely intelligible."[45] Merlan and Donini, in misinterpreting the maxim in such a way that it assumes as premiss the supreme intelligibility of the productive intellect, provide a partially correct interpretation of this passage.[46] The supreme intelligibility of the productive intellect is not only assumed by Alexander as a premiss of argument; it is also a necessary condition of the causation of intelligibility for other intelligible objects. Notice, however, that Alexander also says, "Other good things are judged good by their contribution to this [i.e., being good]." At first sight, this statement concerning the contribution of good things to being good might be regarded as an abrupt exception to the supposedly Platonic participation of visibles in the supremely visible (i.e., light), or of intelligibles in the supremely intelligible (i.e., the productive intellect). Donini sees in this contribution (*sunteleia*)[47] of good things to goodness merely an attempt on the part of Alexander to distance himself from Middle Platonism.

The notion of contribution should in fact be extended, not only to goodness, but to visibility and intelligibility as well. To understand how this is so, we may look to Alexander's understand-

---

[43] Merlan (1963) 39.

[44] Moraux (1942) 90-92.

[45] Lloyd (1976) 150.

[46] See Merlan (1963) and Donini (1974); cf. Schroeder (1981) and (1984). See now the comprehensive review of Alexander's doctrine of intellect in Sharples (1987) 1204-1214.

[47] Donini (1974) 47; for *sunteleia* see Alexander *De Anima* 89.4.

ing, not of light as a term of an analogy, but of light itself. For Alexander *De Anima* 42.19-43.11, illumination is a joint effect produced both by the source of light and by the illumined object. In this pattern of causation the source, by being supremely visible, is the cause of visibility in the illumined object. Yet the illumined object may be regarded as making its own contribution to the production of visibility when the illumined object and the source of light are juxtaposed, i.e., the presence of the illumined object is necessary but (in the absence of the source of light) not a sufficient condition of illumination.

That Alexander's understanding of illumination is not really Platonic (or at least not Neoplatonic) in character may be seen from Plotinus' polemic against it.[48] Plotinus sees illumination as uniquely a product of the *illuminans,* with no need for juxtaposition with nor for contribution from the *illuminatum* ; that is, the *illuminans* is alone both the necessary and the sufficient condition of illumination.

Plotinus, describing the relationship between the One and Intellect, makes use of an analogy of light that seems to owe a philosophical debt to the Aristotelian analogy of the productive intellect to light at *De Anima* 3.5, 430a14-17. Plotinus may further have consulted Alexander's interpretation of the Aristotelian analogy of the productive intellect to light. Now we have seen how the Plotinian theory of illumination differs from Alexander's treatment of this subject. For Plotinus, illumination is uniquely the product of the source, while for Alexander it is a joint effect proceeding both from the source of light and the illumined object. We may reasonably expect that these differences will be reflected in the analogy of light used by these authors. Indeed Plotinus, in invoking the analogy of light to describe the relationship between the One and Intellect, stresses the role of the One as the source of intellection and intelligibility in a manner which reflects his understanding of the source of light as unique

---

[48] See Alexander *De Anima* 42.19-43.11, Plotinus 4.5 [29].7.33-49 and Schroeder (1984).

cause of illumination. Thus the role of the source here offers a parallel to the part played by the source of light in the Plotinian physics of light. In Alexander's use of the analogy of light, as we have observed, intelligibility and intellection are a joint effect proceeding from both the productive intellect and the objects of thought, even as both the source of light and the illumined objects are required for there to be illumination.[49]

It should, however, be observed that for Plotinus (even though he may employ predication *per eminentiam*), it is not simply the case that the cause must possess to the supreme degree the character of its effect. Indeed Plotinus is concerned to understand how the One can produce that which is *not* itself.[50] Thus the One, while it is the supreme object of thought, is object of thought for Intellect, but is not intrinsically an object of thought.[51]

For Alexander, just as light, by being supremely visible, is the cause of visibility, so also is the productive intellect, as supreme object of thought, the cause for other objects of thought of their being such objects of thought in turn. Yet these make their own contribution to this effect when they are brought into juxtaposition with the productive intellect that is supremely an object of thought. How and where does this take place? Alexander traces the psychic hierarchy extending from the first supervention of the soul on corporeal mixture (25.2-3) to the dawn of intellection (80.16-24), through to the advance from imagination, to memory and on to the abstraction and appropriation of the immanent enmattered forms that are potentially objects of thought (83.2-84.9). Now there are, in Alexander, two classes of forms, objects of thought: immaterial or transcendent and enmattered or immanent. The immaterial or transcendent forms that are objects of thought are eternal and are identical with the act of thinking them on the part of the productive intellect that thinks them

---

[49] Cf. Plotinus 4.5 [29].7; 5.1 [10].6; 6.7 [38].16 and Schroeder (1984) 244-248.

[50] See Plotinus 5.3 [49].15.35; 6.7 [38].15.19; 6.7 [38].17.4 and Schroeder (1984); Plotinus 5.1 [10].7 and Schroeder (1986).

[51] See Plotinus 5.6 [24].2.7-21 and Schroeder (1984) 247.

always.[52] These forms, by being supremely intelligible, are the ultimate cause for the enmattered or immanent forms, both of their being objects of thought and of their being (89.7-11). Yet these enmattered forms do not exist qua objects of thought until they are abstracted by the human mind (90.2-9; 84.19-21). Thus the human intelligence is the *locus* of that juxtaposition of immanent and transcendent forms, objects of thought which is necessary to metaphysical illumination.[53]

If we construe the formula, *propter quod alia, id maximum tale* to mean that it is by possessing an attribute to the highest degree that the source is the cause of the existence of that same attribute (although in lesser degree) in its products, then that formula does not describe the production either of illumination or of human intellection in Alexander. If we are to think that this maxim expresses Platonism, then Alexander, as he does not observe it, is not at Platonist. Furthermore, Alexander is not poised on the brink of Neoplatonism. If Plotinus, the father of Neoplatonism, is a Platonist, in the sense that he stresses that illumination is uniquely the product of its source, then he exhibits a profound difference from Alexander for whom illumination is a joint effect proceeding both from the source of illumination and the illumined object. The difference between these authors concerning the nature of illumination is, as we have seen, reflected in their use of the analogy of light in explaining the genesis of intellection. The use of the formula, *propter quod alia, id maximum tale* to

---

[52] *De Anima* 88.2 *aülon eidos* (immaterial form); 87.29 *noêta ta enula* (enmattered form). See Todd (1976) 210 and 216. For a discussion of the question whether transcendent of immaterial form, object of thought, is singular or plural, see Commentary at 108.14. For the relationship between the productive intellect and its objects, see 90.11-13 and Merlan (1967) 118; see also 88.3-5 and Merlan (1969) 39 where Merlan argues correctly that the productive intellect produces the immaterial or the transcendent forms, objects of thought, by thinking them eternally. It is said to be the cause of all objects of thought (89.10-11).

[53] The human mind enters into identity with the enmattered or immanent forms, or objects of thought (87.29-88.10; 90.2-4; 84.22-24). The human mind may also enter into some kind of identity with the productive intellect (89.21-91.6); Schroeder (1981) 224.

compare Alexander and Plotinus is further faulted by its inapplicability to Plotinus, who does not think that the source, by the fact of possessing an attribute to the highest degree, is the cause of that attribute for its products.[54]

Moraux in 1942 distinguished between an *esprit métaphysique* and an *esprit scientifique* in Alexander. He viewed the naturalistic account of the rise of thought in Alexander as sufficient without the supervention of the productive intellect, an unnecessary item of metaphysical baggage.[55] We may now see that there is rather a grand design in which the natural and metaphysical orders meet when the human mind advances to the omega point of noetic illumination.

The *De Intellectu,* with its stilted list of the phases of intellect and its wooden presentation of the argument, stands in sharp contrast with the *De Anima* of Alexander. Nowhere may its deficiencies be seen more clearly than in the way in which it draws the analogy of the productive intellect to light. At 107.31 we read:

> For *as* light becomes for colours that are potentially visible the cause of their becoming actually visible, *so also* does this third intellect make the potential and material intellect intellect in actuality by producing a state where thought is possessed.

The analogy is at best elliptical. Surely to the colours that are seen (i.e., to visible objects), there should correspond, not intellect in the state of possession, but objects of thought. What is more, the very use of ordinal numerals, as in "third intellect," reads like a set of notes, something which is derivative and imperfectly understood. The second occurrence of the analogy to light (111.32), while an improvement over this, is still deficient.[56]

Donini, as has been shown, argues that the *De Intellectu* should be relegated to Alexander's juvenalia.[57] We have already observed

---

[54] Schroeder (1984).

[55] Moraux (1942) 48-49 and especially 49 note 1. Movia (1970a) provides a useful review of scholarship on the question of these two tendencies in the thought of Alexander.

[56] See Commentary *ad loc.*

[57] Donini (1974) 59-62.

that the noetic doctrine of the *De Intellectu,* while it betrays
similarities to the philosophy of mind in Alexander's *De Anima,*
seems unoriginal. It would surely be more economical to argue
that this material was derived from the mature work of Alexander
than to maintain that Alexander built the edifice of his mature
work upon his own youthful writings, if these were themselves
borrowed from some other source.

There are, of course, undeniable similarities between the *De
Anima* and the *De Intellectu.* But because of the great divergence
of doctrine on the role of the productive intellect in producing
human thought, it is hard to see from what source these similarities would arise, especially in the absence of overt polemic. This
difference is also difficult to explain on the grounds of intellectual
development in one author. If we knew more of the intellectual
history of Alexander's period, we might better understand and be
able to account for the similarities and differences.[58] But failing
that we must seriously doubt whether the *De Intellectu* is an
authentic part of the Alexandrian corpus.

Besides the body of commentaries and monographs that form
the established Alexandrian corpus, there are two collections
both of which Moraux regarded as of questionable authenticity,
the *De Anima Mantissa* and the *Quaestiones.*[59] The *De Anima
Mantissa* is the uncomplimentary title the editor Bruns assigned
to the collection of writings appended to the *De Anima* proper
(*mantissa* means "supplement" or "makeweight").[60] Of the
twenty-five items of which this collection consists, only the first
five undertake a direct engagement with psychology. This second
De Anima doubtless owes its title, not to the importance of these

---

[58] The terms "potential intellect" and "intellect in actuality" occur at
Alcinous *Didaskalikos* p. 164 Hermann (on the authorship of this work see
Commentary at 108.14), although these terms bear a very different sense from
their meaning in Alexander (see Ballériaux 84). The view that the soul is a
dunamis that is to be identified with or which supervenes upon corporeal fusion
doubtless antedates Alexander (see notes 32 and 33 above).

[59] Moraux (1942) 140-141.

[60] Sharples (1983) 16.

writings, but to their position at the beginning of the book.[61] The other writings treat of vision and light, physics, ethics and the Peripatetic doctrines of fate and providence.

The *Quaestiones,* in four books, appears to be a disparate and crudely compiled collection (including psychological material).[62] Moraux advanced the view that the psychological treatises of the *Mantissa* belong in the same collection with the *Quaestiones* which similarly includes psychological treatises among writings addressed to other topics. [63] He also considers the *Quaestiones* themselves of doubtful authenticity as works of Alexander himself.[64] If we so regard the psychological writings of the *Quaestiones* and further see the psychological treatises of the *Mantissa* as belonging together with them, we may have further reason for doubting Alexander's authorship of the *De Intellectu.*[65]

Thillet, in his introduction to his edition and translation of the *De Fato,* objects that to regard all these minor writings as inauthentic or as works of Alexander's disciples is a dangerous enterprise that may invite us to reject truly authentic works.[66] The *De Fato,* the authenticity of which is undoubted, follows immediately upon the treatise on fate at the end of the *Mantissa* in codex *Venetus Marcianus graecus* 258. Thillet argues that if Moraux's doubts with respect to the *De Intellectu* are extended to the whole collection, then the *De Fato* would also come under suspicion (he advances the same sort of arguments with respect to the *De Providentia,* which is also known to be by Alexander).[67] Moraux, however, does not simply find the *Quaestiones* suspect by their

---

[61] Moraux (1942) 27.

[62] Bruns v-ix; Moraux (1942) 19-28.

[63] Moraux (1942) 28. In Moraux's view, the greatest difference between the psychological treatises of the *Mantissa* and those of the *Quaestiones* is that the former address themselves more directly to themes encountered in Alexander himself; the latter, while they have affinities with Alexander's thought, address themselves more directly to Aristotelian texts.

[64] Moraux (1942) 22.

[65] Ibid., (1942) 140-141.

[66] Thillet (1984) liii-liv.

[67] Ibid., liv-lv.

association with the *De Intellectu,* but discovers internal reasons
for his doubts with respect to their authenticity. They are related
to the greater works of Alexander, yet add nothing.[68]

Aristotle of Mytilene and the De Intellectu

At 110.4 we encounter a crux that has an important bearing on
questions surrounding the *De Intellectu:*"Ηκουσα δὲ περὶ νοῦ
τοῦ θύραθεν παρὰ † 'Αριστοτέλους, ἃ διεσωσάμην. This will
admit of the translation: "I heard concerning the intellect from
without from Aristotle those things that I have preserved." Zeller,
in the face of the entire Greek manuscript tradition, emended
'Αριστοτέλους (the genitive of "Aristotle") to 'Αριστοκλέους
(the genitive of "Aristocles"), chiefly on the grounds that the
Stoicizing doctrine evident in 112.5 to 113.24 could not belong
to the Stagirite.[69] His argument seems to assume that ἀκούειν
παρά and the genitive (the combination of verb, preposition and
case rendered by "hear concerning") cannot refer to anything but
contemporary oral instruction. He also found precedents for the
corruption of "Aristocles" to "Aristotle." Believing that the *De
Intellectu* was a work of Alexander of Aphrodisias and being
unable to find a contemporary of Alexander of the name of
Aristotle, Zeller took it that Aristocles of Messene, of whom we
have fragments from Eusebius,[70] was the teacher of Alexander.

Moraux criticized Zeller for finding Aristocles only in the
second of the discussions introduced at 110.4;[71] that is, in the
material from 112.5ff. and ignoring the first discussion extending

---

[68] Moraux (1942) 22.

[69] Zeller 814 note 1; 815 note 3. For the previous history of the view that
Aristocles was the teacher of Alexander see Moraux (1967) 170-173; (1984)
399-401. The original basis for the view that the referent is Aristocles is to be
found in the Latin version of Simplicius *In De Caelo* by William of Moerbeke
where Alexander appears to refer to Aristocles as his teacher. This was re-
translated into Greek in the Aldine edition of the Greek text. The Greek
manuscripts refer to "Aristotle," cf. Simplicius *In De Caelo* (CAG 7) 153.17 and
Moraux (1967) 170 and note 3.

[70] See Heiland.

[71] Moraux (1942) 142-149.

from 110.4-112.5. The first discussion gives a fully adequate account of how the productive intellect is present in us by being an object of thought for us. Thus the Stoicizing[72] comment concerning the ubiquity of intellect provided at 112.5ff. is unnecessary. At 110.5-6 the author gives us an account of the considerations said to move Aristotle to introduce the intellect from without. This account is introduced by the impersonal "were said to be" (τὰ γὰρ κινήσαντα ... ἐλέγετο εἶναι); the impersonal construction is resumed at 110.24-25). If the reference were to a specific teacher of Alexander, we would expect a personal construction. The doctrine of 110.4-112.5 is Alexandrian and need not be explained by reference to Aristocles. What is more, the Stoicizing material from 112.5 to the end does not fit with anything that we know of Aristocles of Messene. Most important, however, is Moraux's lexicographical argument[73] that ἤκουσα παρὰ 'Αριστοτέλους need not mean, "I heard from the mouth of Aristotle," but can bear the more general sense, "I learned from Aristotle," that is, "by a tradition which makes Aristotelian claims." This would better fit with the impersonal construction that follows. Moraux translates: "J'ai eu conaissance d'une théorie d'Aristote sur l'intellect extérieur, et je l'ai conservée fidèlement."[74]

The second discussion, which extends from 112.5 to the end, is introduced by personal verbs of saying (ἔλεγε, ἔφασκε).[75] What is the subject of these verbs? The teaching they introduce is opposed to that of Alexander himself. They cannot refer to Aristotelian teaching generally, as the impersonal construction at 110.5-6 does. They must therefore refer to a distinct alternative source. The section begins with a participle with no proper referent ("wishing" [βουλόμενος] at 112.5). Moraux supposes a lacuna before this participle.[76]

---

[72] On the Stoicizing content of this passage, see Commentary at 112.9.
[73] Moraux (1942) 148.
[74] Moraux (1942) 148; 189.
[75] See 112.8,10; 113.2,5.
[76] Moraux (1942) 148-149.

Trabucco, like Zeller, detected reference to Aristocles of Messene at 110.4 and made it the basis for a reconstruction (comparing Alexander of Aphrodisias with the known fragments of Aristocles). Indeed, that the reference at 110.4 was to Aristocles had by 1967 become *communis opinio.*[77] Now an important consideration for Zeller was that there was no known contemporary of Alexander of Aphrodisias named Aristotle. This was one of the reasons that compelled him to resort to emendation. Moraux, however, found a reference in Galen[78] in which the great physician speaks of an Aristotle of Mytilene as a prominent Peripatetic. Moraux argues in this later article that chronology would allow that this Aristotle of Mytilene was the teacher of Alexander. Obviously it is better to avoid textual emendation. Moraux therefore abandons his earlier position on the lexicography of *akouein para* and the genitive and insists emphatically that there is no instance of the phrase in question referring to anything other than contemporary oral instruction.

It is crucial to observe that this lexicographical argument attaches, not to *akouein* generally, but to *akouein para* and the genitive. The verb *akouein* and the genitive (in the absence of *para*) may, by an extension of the classical sense of "listen," admit the meaning "to interpret, understand" and refer to a philosopher who is not a contemporary.[79] Thillet is unable to find an example of *akouein para* and the genitive as referring to anything other

---

[77] Trabucco (1958); Moraux (1967) 172 note 6.

[78] Galen *De Consuetudinibus (Peri Ethôn)* ed. I. Müller (*Galeni Scripta Minora* vol. 2 [Leipzig: 1891]) 11.4-5; Moraux (1967) 176-177.

[79] Plotinus 4.8 [6].4.39; 2.9 [33].17.2; 2.1 [40].7.1 uses the verb thus of Plato. Themistius, correcting an interpretation of Aristotle put forth by Alexander, invites us to "hear" Aristotle and, in answering the opponents of one of his interpretations, invites us to "hear Aristotle crying aloud" (*In De Anima* 102.34). This sense occurs in Alexander *De Mixtione* 216.10; *In Analytica Priora* (CAG 2.1) 60.9; 309.11; 369.4; *In De Sensu* (CAG 3.1) 171.26; *In Topica* (CAG 2.2) 253.23 and instances may easily be multiplied for its use by later Aristotelian commentators by an examination of the word indices of the *Commentaria in Aristotelem Graeca.* For instances of *akouein* as "read" referring to persons whom one could not have heard, see Goulet 407 note 6.

than contemporary oral instruction. He does, however, find in Plutarch an instance of *akouein para* and the dative in the sense of "to learn from having read" and asks whether *akouein para* and the genitive might not bear the same sense.[80] As he admits, however, this is rather a rash hypothesis in the absence of any specific examples.

Moraux also discovers four apparent references to an Aristotle as teacher of Alexander of Aphrodisias from the fifth and sixth centuries AD.[81] Thillet undertakes a careful examination of the four passages in question and advances cogent arguments against the necessity of our seeing in any of these a reference to Aristotle of Mytilene as Moraux assumed.[82] In 1985 Moraux claimed to discover a further reference to Aristotle (*sc.* of Mytilene) as teacher of Alexander in Alexander's commentary on the *Metaphysics* and tells us that, in private correspondence, Thillet has informed him that, had he examined this most recent piece of evidence, he would have been more open to Moraux's idea.[83] Indeed Accattino, independently of Moraux, also discovered a reference to Aristotle of Mytilene in this passage (although he offers convincing argument against Moraux's location of such a reference in Syrianus).

In the second volume of his major study of the Greek reception of Aristotle,[84] Moraux, without knowing Thillet's work, expands upon his paper of 1967 to give an analysis of *De Intellectu* 110.4-113.24 on the assumption that the reference at 110.4 is to Aristotle of Mytilene, teacher of Alexander of Aphrodisias. At

---

[80] Thillet (1984) xvi-xvii; see also xvii note 1 where he refers to Plutarch *Quomodo adolescens poetas audire debeat* 14, *Moralia* 36e and 37a, ed. W.R. Paton and I. Wegehaupt, rev. H. Gärtner (Teubner ed. 1974) 1:75.3-4.

[81] The texts advanced by Moraux are Cyril of Alexandria *Contra Iulianum* (*Patrologia Graeca* 76) 2.596a; 5.704b; 5.741a; Simplicius *In De Caelo* (CAG 7) 153.11-154.5; Elias *In Categorias* (CAG 18.1) 128.10-13; Syrianus *In Metaphysica* (CAG 6.1) 100.6.

[82] See Thillet (1984) xi-xxxi; Thillet had not yet seen Moraux (1984). Martorana gives an uncritical report of Moraux (1967).

[83] Alexander *In Metaphysica* (CAG 1) 166.19-20; Moraux (1985) 269.

[84] Moraux (1984) 399-425.

110.5-6, as we have seen, an impersonal construction introduces the reasons why Aristotle advanced the doctrine of the intellect from without. This impersonal construction is repeated at 110.24-25 to remind us that these were the considerations that motivated Aristotle to formulate this doctrine. Then from 110.25 to 112.5 there is further examination of the intellect from without and of human thought and the relationship between the intellect from without and the human intellect. Then at 112.5 we read: "Wishing to show that intellect was immortal and to escape the problems that they raise for the intellect from without ... according to his own reflection, he said the following concerning the intellect that is said to exist in the whole of the mortal body." Now, whatever we may wish to say about the body of doctrine preceding this statement, the teaching advanced after 112.5 is of such a character that it cannot possibly be referred to Aristotle the Stagirite.[85] That is to say that the participle "wishing" is left without a proper referent. As we have seen, Moraux in 1942 had supposed a lacuna.

In his later study, Moraux, of course, finds a convenient referent for the participle at 112.5 in the Aristotle (*sc.* of Mytilene) at 110.4. The impersonal constructions at 110.5-6 and 110.24-25 Moraux takes to refer to Aristotle of Mytilene.[86] The passage from 110.4 to 112.5 presents a common tradition concerning the intellect from without to which Aristotle of Mytilene subscribed. The passage at 112.5 represents, in contrast with this inherited material, the peculiar views of Aristotle of Mytilene.[87]

---

[85] Ibid., 412.

[86] Ibid.

[87] Sharples (1986) 33-34 argues against the view of Thillet (1984) that the third person references at 110.5, giving an account of why Aristotle introduced the intellect from without and at 112.5, providing the arguments against it, could both refer to the Stagirite: "It is one thing to read an interpretation into a text, but quite another to describe the text as explicitly commenting in the third person on its own author's motives." Sharples (1987) 1203 note 81; 1211-1212; 1216 supports Moraux's prosopographical identification.

Thillet points out that there are in the *De Intellectu* several references to Aristotle the Stagirite.[88] If the reference at 110.4 is to an Aristotle other than the Stagirite, it must seem strange that the author would not attempt to avoid the confusion this homonymy must introduce. The impersonal construction at 110.5-6 (resumed at 110.24-25) ill suits reference to such a figure. An active verb would be more natural. There is also evidence that an ancient pupil could be most zealous in his claim to have inside knowledge of his master's teachings and that, in so doing, would speak in the first person.[89] Thillet objects that Alexander cites his teachers Herminus and Sosigenes several times.[90] It is therefore peculiar that this should be the only reference to this teacher by Alexander himself. This argument would, of course, be disarmed if with Moraux we see a reference to Aristotle of Mytilene in Alexander's commentary on the *Metaphysics*. On the other hand, that reference will itself be a unique occurrence if we doubt, as we reasonably can, that Alexander is the author of the *De Intellectu*. What is more, in the text in which Moraux finds what is supposed to be a secure reference by Alexander himself to an Aristotle other than the Stagirite (*In Metaphysica* [CAG 1] 166.19-20), Alexander appears to distinguish the latter-day Aristotle from the Stagirite by referring to him as "our Aristotle" (ἡμέτερος 'Αριστοτέλης). If there is reference to such a figure at 110.4, why does such a phrase not appear here, to distinguish between the two Aristotles?

This is to introduce another troubling question about this exercise in prosopography. The argument that Aristotle of Mytilene was the teacher of Alexander of Aphrodisias depends upon the assumption that the *De Intellectu* is a work from the hand of Alexander. The chronological considerations that invite us to identify a reference to Aristotle of Mytilene in this document also depend upon this assumption. What is more, the value of

---

[88] Thillet (1984) xvii.
[89] For the evidence, see Commentary at 110.5.
[90] Thillet (1984) xvii.

other references to an Aristotle other than the Stagirite as teacher of Alexander can only contribute to the prosopography of 110.4 if we assume that the *De Intellectu* was written by Alexander. We have already offered argument that the authorship of this work is, at the very least, not a question which has been definitely settled. It is, as we have seen, crucial to the success of Moraux's argument, that *akouein para* with the genitive can only bear reference to contemporary oral instruction. But in light of our reservations about authenticity, Moraux's prosopography seems, apart from this evidence of language and the questionable identification of an Aristotle in later texts, to lack a firm foundation.

Perhaps there is a solution along other lines. Let us examine two titles from the *De Anima Mantissa*:

(1) τῶν παρὰ 'Αριστοτέλους περὶ τοῦ πρώτου οἰκείου ("[Selections] from Aristotle concerning what is first endeared to us"), 150.19.

(2) τῶν παρὰ 'Αριστοτέλους περὶ τοῦ ἐφ' ἡμῖν ("[Selections] from Aristotle concerning what is in our power"), 169.33 and 172.16.[91]

In each of these, the phrase τὰ παρὰ 'Αριστοτέλους means "the views derived from Aristotle." At Plato *Theaetetus* 148e2-3 Theaetetus describes himself as ἀκούων τὰς παρὰ σοῦ ἀποφερομένας ἐρωτήσεις. McDowell renders this: "When I've heard *reports* [italics ours] of your questions." Here παρὰ σοῦ is the equivalent of σάς and it would be artificial to take it as a personal agent phrase with ἀποφερομένας. Similarly then παρὰ 'Αριστοτέλους can be construed as "Aristotelian" in the titles from the *Mantissa*. We may also compare Themistius *In De Anima* 38.34-35: ἃ μὲν παρὰ τῶν πρότερον εἴχομεν παραδεδομένα περὶ ψυχῆς εἴρηται ("What was handed down from the prede-

---

[91] Sharples (1986) 33, while disagreeing with the arguments of Thillet (1984) against Moraux's identification of the "Aristotle" of 110.4 with Aristotle of Mytilene, seems briefly to suggest that the latter two titles might support Thillet's view. He overlooks 150.19. See now Sharples (1987) 1211 note 131.

cessors [of Aristotle] concerning the soul has been discussed").
Here again παρά and the genitive convey the sense of a tradition.
Notice also that this phrase is conjoined, as at *De Intellectu* 110.4,
with περί and the genitive.
Now let us return to *De Intellectu* 110.4 where we again
encounter the phrase παρὰ 'Αριστοτέλους. Suppose that we
read: ἤκουσα δὲ <τὰ> περὶ νοῦ θύραθεν παρὰ 'Αριστοτέλους. We could translate: "I heard <the> [views] on the intellect
from without from [derived from] Aristotle—." In so doing we
invoke the sense of παρὰ 'Αριστοτέλους, expressed elsewhere
in the *Mantissa*, as "derived from Aristotle."[92] In each of the
Mantissa titles examined, then, the phrase τὰ παρὰ 'Αριστοτέλους means "the views derived from Aristotle." Obviously the
opinions described need not be those of Aristotle himself, since
the very vocabulary of these titles is Stoic.[93]
This means that we are returning to something very like the
position Moraux had advanced in 1942. Closer again is a view
expressed by Moraux in private communication in 1961 where
the following translation is offered: "Au sujet de la théorie
aristotélicienne de l'intellect venu du dehors, j'ai entendu propo-
ser des explications que j'ai tenu à conserver."[94] This gets the
force of παρὰ 'Αριστοτέλους as "views derived from Aristotle"
better than did his earlier translation: "J'ai eu connaissance d'une
théorie d'Aristote sur l'intellect extérieur, et je l'ai conservée
fidèlement."[95] Thus παρὰ 'Αριστοτέλους would admit the
translation "Aristotelian." Moraux's translation of 1961 would,
however, demand our emendation <τὰ> παρὰ 'Αριστοτέλους

---

[92] At *Mantissa* 113.27 we do encounter δείκνυται παρὰ 'Αριστοτέλους.
Here παρά is equivalent to ὑπό. It would surely, however, be artificial to
interpret 110.4 as ἤκουσα δὲ τὰ περὶ νοῦ τοῦ θύραθεν παρὰ 'Αριστοτέλους δειχθέντα. It is better to take παρὰ 'Αριστοτέλους as equivalent to
'Αριστοτελικά.
[93] See Adler's *Index Verborum* svf 4 under ἐφ' ἡμῖν and πρῶτον οἰκεῖον.
The τῶν παρὰ 'Αριστοτέλους περὶ τοῦ ἐφ' ἡμῖν (*Mantissa* 169.35-172.15)
is hardly orthodox Aristotelianism; cf. Sharples (1975) 42-52.
[94] Carrière *et al.* 27 note 22.
[95] Moraux (1942) 189.

and this may in itself be considered an objection. Moraux's revised translation does have the advantage that it evades emendation altogether. Nevertheless the emendation is slight and yields a simple and not unconvincing alternative to the complex argument of Moraux's later discussions.

The sentence at 110.4, however interpreted, betrays resemblances to the form of titles that occur elsewhere in the *Mantissa*. One might be almost tempted to see in it, if we were to remove the first two and the last two words, a kind of title, *viz.* "Concerning the intellect from without from Aristotle." Admittedly the παρὰ ᾿Αριστοτέλους ("from Aristotle") comes after the prepositional phrase "on the intellect from without," whereas in the titles it comes before. Perhaps then we should avoid that temptation.

Let us look now at the overall structure of the *De Intellectu* in light of this discussion. The material from 106.19-110.3 can certainly stand on its own. Assuming a lacuna before 112.5, the account of the intellect from without from 110.4 to 112.5 may also be seen as an independent work.

The use of the first person "I heard" as at 110.4 is very unusual in Greek Aristotelian commentaries. Indeed, the first person singular is usual only in texts such as the dedication to the *De Fato* of Alexander or in Themistius' proem to his paraphrase of the *Posterior Analytics*.[96] Normally the first person plural, or an impersonal construction, is the means by which a commentator conveys his views. Indeed at 110.4 we have two instances of the first person singular in ἤκουσα and διεσωσάμην. This peculiarity would in itself be a strong argument for regarding the material from 110.4 to 112.5 (assuming a lacuna at 112.5) as an independent work. It is worth noting that the two instances of the first person in Alexander and Themistius cited above are used in introductions. Such a use of the first person singular at 110.4 might then serve to initiate an independent text that would reach to 112.5.

[96] See Alexander *De Fato* (sa 2.2) 164.3, 9; Themistius *In Analytica Posteriora* 1.2.

If we do suppose a lacuna before 112.5, then we are left with a truncated fragment at the end of the *De Intellectu.* We may note, however, that any lacuna placed before the participle "wishing" at 112.5 would not be unparalleled in the *Mantissa.*[97] It further appears that material at 113.18-24 would more logically belong at 112.5-11.[98] If this text is transposed, we may have more reason to believe that the text is in general badly compiled and have less reason to be surprised at the lack of a referent for the participle at 112.5. We have already, in the last section, had occasion to observe that the *Mantissa,* like the *Quaestiones,* may be regarded as a badly compiled collection.

It may be possible, then, to oppose to Moraux's unitarian position an analytic argument that would question, not only the authorship, but the unity of the *De Intellectu* so that it would now have to be seen as two distinct treatises and a fragment of a third. This solution may be regarded as unsatisfactory. It might, however, be preferable to tolerate such a result than to accept that from the ashes of Aristocles of Messene there should emerge the noetic of Aristotle of Mytilene.

2. THEMISTIUS' PARAPHRASE OF ARISTOTLE *DE ANIMA* 3.4-8

Historical Importance of the Themistian Noetic

The paraphrase of Aristotle's *De Anima* by Themistius (AD 317?-388?) is one of five such commentaries by this author that are extant.[99] Its authenticity is guaranteed by numerous references

---

[97] See *Mantissa* 102.9, with Bruns *ad loc.*

[98] See Commentary *ad loc.*

[99] Three survive in Greek (CAG 5.1-3), on the *Posterior Analytics, Physics,* and *De Anima,* while two, on the *De Caelo* and *Metaphysics Lambda,* survive in Hebrew versions (CAG 5.4 and 5). I shall cite that on *Metaphysics Lambda* from the Latin translation that accompanies the Hebrew text at CAG 5.5. There is a partial version of it in Arabic edited by Badawi (1947), parts of which are translated and discussed by Pines (1987). Blumenthal (1979a) is an important demonstration against Steel that Themistius did not write Aristotelian commentaries in addition to the paraphrases. Some of Themistius' Aristotelian exegeses have not survived. His work on Aristotle's *Topica,* for example, was known to Boethius and Ibn Rushd; see Stump 212-213.

in later Greek commentaries.[100] In terms of influence it is undoubtedly his most important work. After antiquity it was translated into Arabic by Isḥāq ibn Ḥunain (d. AD 910),[101] and subsequently became known to thirteenth century western thinkers[102] both from quotations in Averroes' commentary on the *De Anima*,[103] and through William of Moerbeke's translation from Greek into Latin.[104] It continued to be studied in the fifteenth and sixteenth centuries when there were some new translations.[105]

This influence resulted principally from parts of the material translated here. Themistius offered an interpretation of Aristotle's account of the so called active, or productive, intellect[106] in *De Anima* 3.5 that rejected the identification of that intellect with the Aristotelian God proposed by his predecessor Alexander of Aphrodisias.[107] Themistius could also be read as positing indi-

---

[100] Some of these are discussed in Blumenthal (1979a).

[101] It is at least attributed to him in the one extant manuscript. See Lyons (1955), and the introduction to Lyons (1973) vii-xi. For its significance for the constitution of the Greek text see Browne *passim*. On Themistius' general Arabic *fortuna* see Peters (1968a) 40 and 42, and Badawi 100-103.

[102] On St. Thomas Aquinas' use of Moerbeke's translation see the introduction to Verbeke (1957) i-lxii, where earlier literature is cited. On Themistius' wider influence in the thirteenth century on such thinkers as Siger of Brabant, Henry Bate of Malines, and James of Viterbo see Mahoney (1973) and (1982b). These studies contain extensive references to earlier scholarly literature.

[103] See Hyman 177-180 on Ibn Rushd's use of Themistius.

[104] Edited by Verbeke (1957).

[105] See Mahoney (1973) 427 for details. That by Ermolao Barbaro, first published in 1481, has recently been reprinted; see Lohr. Mahoney (1982a) 170-173 discusses Themistius' influence in the Renaissance.

[106] Although the term "active intellect" is in common use, it has no direct Aristotelian equivalent, and is really a mistranslation of the commentators' term *poiêtikos nous* which we have consistently rendered as "productive intellect." In discussing Themistius' interpretations the terms "productive intellect" and "actual intellect" (or "intellect in actuality") will be used, depending on which is dominant in any given context. "Actual intellect" has the virtue of being firmly contrasted with "potential intellect" (or "intellect in potentiality"), while implying that an activity is involved in this actuality. At 99.32-100.15 Themistius, in fact, explicitly sets out a description of the productive intellect in terms of its actuality and activity.

[107] 102.36-103.19; Alexander is not mentioned by name in this passage.

vidual productive intellects.[108] In the theological context that surrounded the medieval exegesis of the Aristotelian noetic such interpretations not surprisingly interested and influenced a number of thinkers.

Biography and Significance of Themistius[109]

Themistius was born at Constantinople around AD 317 into an aristocratic family from Paphlagonia. His father, Eugenius, himself a philosopher, ensured that his son was educated both in rhetoric and in a wide range of philosophical doctrines, though he did not bring him into contact with any major centres of philosophy. Themistius eventually administered his own school at Constantinople between about 345 and 355, and it was probably during this period that most of his Aristotelian paraphrases were composed.[110] He subsequently entered on a long political and diplomatic career at the imperial court of Constantinople, and this is reflected in the numerous public orations from which his biography can be reconstructed in some detail.[111] In the Greek world his influence is evident in Aristotelian commentaries of later antiquity. In Byzantium it continued both through his paraphrases and orations; indeed the Byzantine penchant for Aristotelian paraphrase may well owe its origin to his style of exegesis.[112]

Themistius lived in a century in which the dominant philosophical movement was an elaborated form of Platonism. He did not,

---

[108] On this issue see below 103.32-33 and note 121.

[109] On Themistius' life and philosophical works see the general accounts in Stegemann 1642-1648 and 1651-1655 (earlier literature cited at 1648); Überweg-Prächter 656-658; Faggin; Dagron 5-16; Jones *et al.* 889-894; Verbeke (1976); Mahoney (1973) 424 and Mahoney (1982a) 169 note 1.

[110] *In De Anima* 39.23 offers the clearest evidence of a link between the paraphrases and oral teaching.

[111] Passages from these orations sometimes throw light on Themistius' commentaries, but because of their context need careful evaluation. No attempt will be made to exploit them in the present study.

[112] Cf. Sophonias (s. xiii) *In De Anima* (CAG 23.1) 1.20-21 for favourable comment on Themistius' method.

however, assimilate its ideas systematically into his surviving works. His Aristotelian paraphrases are too closely based on the text to allow for the kind of reconstructions that later Neoplatonic commentators were to formulate as a matter of principle. At the same time his orations, and on occasion his paraphrases, reveal an acquaintance with the Platonic corpus that is unmediated by Neoplatonic exegesis.[113] Themistius' relationship to the twin pillars of the ancient philosophical tradition is, therefore, unusually free from scholasticism. In this we can perhaps detect the intellectual independence of an aristocrat whose involvement with teaching was a relatively brief prelude to a public career and not a lifelong professional commitment.[114]

This picture of Themistius' philosophical background does, however, need some qualification when his account of Aristotle's theory of the intellect is examined in detail. Although he cannot be said to offer a Neoplatonic reading of this doctrine, his text, as we shall see, contains Plotinian parallels and echoes that indicate an interest in Neoplatonism otherwise absent from his works.[115]

---

[113] On the orations see Blumenthal (1979b) 392-393. The quotations from Plato in Themistius' commentaries are similarly drawn directly from his works; in the material translated here cf. 104.3-6, and 106.17-27. Photius *Bibliotheca* Cod. 74 reports that Themistius engaged in "exegetical labours on Platonic matters" (*eis ta Platônika ... exêgetikoi ponoi*). He need not be referring to separate works but to discussions of Platonic texts such as we find at *In De Anima* 19.17-20.18 or 106.15-107.29. For examples of metaphorical language drawn from Platonic dialogues in the material translated here see notes 17, 48, 85, 154, 156, 186, 196 (cf. 228) and 199 to the translation.

[114] Thus even if his paraphrases show him to have been primarily interested in Aristotle it does not follow that he was a representative of "the late Peripatetic school" (Verbeke [1976] 307), or was among "die späteren Peripatetiker" (Überweg-Prächter 656-658), or was "predominantly a Peripatetic" (Blumenthal [1979b] 400). There is no evidence of any formal organization among Peripatetics in the fourth century AD, and none to indicate that Themistius gave his school any institutional affiliation. Also, none of his paraphrases contain passages expressing the sort of doctrinal commitment that we find, for example, in Alexander of Aphrodisias *De Anima* (SA 2.1) 2.4-9, *De Fato* (SA 2.2) 164.13-15, or *De Mixtione* (SA 2.2) 228.5-8.

[115] The evidence for this claim will be presented in notes to the translation;

Paraphrase and Excursus: Themistius' Exposition

Themistius' account of the intellect is part of his paraphrase of Aristotle's account of thinking at *De Anima* 3.4-8, all of which is translated here. This difficult material is usually restated without lengthy digressions, historical addenda, or much internal or external cross-referencing. In some cases Aristotelian texts are simply rephrased, while in others they are more radically transformed and enlarged. In offering this restatement the commentator usually adopts the persona of an Aristotle writing in a more expansive mood.

Themistius may not have originated such an exegetical method but he certainly adapted it for his own purposes.[116] In the proem to his paraphrase of the *Posterior Analytics* he explains that it was not his wish to compete with the major commentaries (*hupomnêmata*) of his predecessors, principally, it can be assumed, those of Alexander of Aphrodisias.[117] Instead he aimed to present parallel restatements of Aristotelian works in order to facilitate a rapid revision of their contents by students unable to recapitulate them with the help of the larger commentaries. This pedagogical goal, reflecting his own career as a teacher, is perhaps best realized in the paraphrase of the *Posterior Analytics* itself. In

---

see especially notes 62, 64, 74-77, 86, 87, 91, 122, 138, 141, 144, 195. Since it involves such a small area of the Themistian corpus, this claim affords no indication of Themistius' philosophical affiliation, or of the form in which he might have had access to Plotinian works. Balleriaux rather overestimated the significance of Plotinian parallels. More recently Blumenthal (1979b) has seen Themistius as a Peripatetic, while Mahoney (1973) and (1982a) has again emphasised the significance of the parallels with Plotinus. Outside the paraphrase of *De Anima* 3.5 Themistius shows acquaintance with an argument of Porphyry at *In De Anima* 25.36-27.7; cf. Moraux (1978a) 307. There is also a parallel between 24.22-25 and Plotinus 4.7 [2].8⁴.11-13, noted by Blumenthal (1971) 11 note 10 who admits that it may reflect use of a common source.

[116] Cf. Blumenthal (1979a) 175 note 28.

[117] *In Analytica Posteriora* 1.1-12. In the paraphrase of the *De Anima* Themistius would seem to be using Alexander's treatise *De Anima* rather than the earlier commentator's lost commentary on the Aristotelian work; he also gives no indication of being acquainted with the *De Intellectu.*

dealing with the *Physics* and *De Anima* Themistius was somewhat more ambitious, though without ever losing sight of his basic goal of providing an account that could, and still can, be easily read in tandem with the Aristotelian text.

In the paraphrase of *De Anima* 3.4-8 this method is followed except for part of the paraphrase of 3.5 where a restatement of most of that chapter (98.10-100.15) is succeeded (at 100.16-109.3) by a radically different type of discussion that is labelled an "excursus" in the present translation.[118] Here the Aristotelian noetic is approached through seven brief discussions that include a programmatic introduction, some problems and solutions, the analysis of parallel Aristotelian texts, and substantial quotations from Plato and Theophrastus. No rationale is offered for this departure, and only at the end (108.35-36) is there some brief indication of its special character. The transitions between the sections are also somewhat abrupt.[119]

The form of this excursus would be of relatively little significance were its content not sometimes difficult to reconcile with that of the paraphrastic sections, largely as a result of its considerably more adventurous approach to textual exegesis.[120] There are, however, no grounds for denying its authenticity, and some evidence to suggest that it was deliberately formulated as an extension of the paraphrase.[121] It should probably be seen as the work of a commentator who in the face of the complexities of *De Anima* 3.5 supplemented a rather pedestrian form of exegesis with a more elaborate reconstruction, without abandoning his method of close textual exegesis. Some of the notes to the translation will deal with the relation between the excursus and its paraphrastic

---

[118] Its special status is acknowledged by, for example, Moraux (1978a) 308, and Blumenthal (1979b) 396. The two modern editors, Spengel and Heinze, treat it as though it is part of an ongoing commentary.

[119] Cf. notes 130 and 133 to the translation.

[120] See especially note 99 to the translation.

[121] Kurfess, 23 note 26, suggested that the excursus contained later additions, but there is evidence of an internal structure to this material (cf. notes 86, 109, 110 to the translation), and also one clear reference back to it in a paraphrastic passage; cf. 109.4-5 with 103.32-33.

context, and evidence will be gathered there to show the links between the two expositions.[122]

Given the complex format of Themistius' exposition, it is difficult to present a synoptic account of his noetic.[123] Interpretation will emerge in discussions in the notes to the translation, but some brief preliminary comments may help to orient the reader.

Themistius is sometimes praised for emphasizing, in contrast with Alexander of Aphrodisias, that the productive intellect is in the human soul (103.4-5, 13), and is not, therefore, identical with the Aristotelian God (102.30-103.19).[124] On this view his noetic seems to be firmly placed in the realm of human psychology. But in fact in the excursus he identifies a suprahuman realm for the intelligizing aspect of the soul. Instead of the activity of the intellect identified in *De Anima* 3.5 being assimilated to the God of *Metaphysics* 12 (*Lambda*), it is linked with the soul by its association, in a compound of form and matter (100.31; 108.32-34; cf. 99.18), with a potential intellect that is its ontological inferior (106.8-9). These intellects can be jointly distinguished from a third intellect (the passive or common intellect: 105.13-34; 108.28-34) that is associated with the functions of memory, emotion and discursive reasoning.[125] It is the latter intellect that is inseparable from the body, while the potential intellect is separate from it (105.26-30), even if less so than the productive intellect because of its more intimate relation to the soul (106.8-14).[126]

---

[122] See, for instance, notes 36, 61, 64, 65 to the translation.

[123] The main general surveys are: Kurfess 19-24; Hamelin 38-43; Nardi 21-25; Verbeke (1957) xxxix-lxii; Davidson 123-124; Mahoney (1973) 428-431 and (1982a) 169 note 1; and Moraux (1978a) 307-313. The fullest modern discussions are by Ballériaux 98-219; S.B. Martin, and Bazán (1976-77).

[124] For example Allan 57-58.

[125] 101.5-102.24; see in particular note 95 to the translation for the untenability of this interpretation, and note 131 for problems involved in distinguishing it from the potential intellect.

[126] On the status of this intellect in the soul cf. note 51 to the translation.

Themistius, therefore, establishes a gulf between God and the soul-related productive intellect, and represents the latter as occupying a suprahuman noetic realm that acts as the guarantor of human reasoning.[127] The potential intellect's separability from the body, and its status as the matter of the productive intellect, is crucial in this reconstruction. This intellect is not merely a precondition for the development of the "acquired" intellect, the state of possessing concepts (95.9-21), but is also the "forerunner" in the soul of the productive intellect (105.30-34), i.e., that which prepares the soul for the kind of thinking that the productive intellect makes possible. However exegetically strange this combination of roles may be,[128] it does mean that the link between the productive intellect and the individual can be represented as a form of self-realization. This is evident in the claim that the essence of the self ("what it is to be me") is the intellect in actuality (100.16-22), and in the interchangeable use of the terms "we" and "productive intellect" (100.37-101.1; 103.16-17). Also, in a passage that builds on Aristotelian texts in rather questionable fashion (101.1-102.24), Themistius develops the view that after death "we," *qua* the productive intellect, do not remember any association with the passive, or common, intellect. Individuality is lost in this collective *noêsis*,[129] just as during life we realize ourselves fully only if we can become identified with this same intellect (cf. 100.18-22). Such self-realization is ensured because the potential intellect from which it arises is eternally associated with the productive intellect (108.32-34).[130] This association does not allow for any change in the productive intellect itself; rather, it establishes the conditions under which the actualization of the potential intellect in an individual soul can occur.

---

[127] Cf. note 119 to the translation..

[128] Kurfess 23 just calls Themistius "obscure" on this point. Cf. notes 51 and 131 to the translation.

[129] On this cf. note 104 to the translation.

[130] It is difficult in the face of this text to see how S.B. Martin 12 can deny that Themistius proposed the immortality of the potential intellect.

Themistius' notion of a collective noetic self preserves the essentials of the Alexandrian identification of the productive intellect and God,[131] insofar as that doctrine identifies a form of self-transcendence. He makes the productive intellect in effect a "second God" in contrast with the "first God" (cf. 102.31, 36; 103.10) that he argues cannot be intended by the intellect introduced in *De Anima* 3.5.[132] Its secondary status lies in its association with the potential intellect, and its wider range of concepts.[133] The "first cause" (as Themistius identifies the Aristotelian God at 112.1) is, on the other hand, "not adapted in the slightest to potentiality" (112.4-5). The Themistian noetic may, therefore, leave the Aristotelian God immune from any association with human intellection, but it still assigns such reasoning its own suprahuman realm. Themistius may have resisted contemporary trends towards a systematic Neoplatonic reading of the *De Anima*, but his misguided exegesis still located Aristotle's account of the intellect in the context of an albeit more modest metaphysical hierarchy and rather less elaborate process of self-realization.

A Note on Presentation

The text translated here is taken from the edition by R. Heinze in the *Commentaria in Aristotelem Graeca.* Any supplements in

[131] Hicks, in his introduction to his edition of the *De Anima* lxv, similarly notes that Themistius' emphasis on the unity of the intellect minimizes his differences with Alexander.

[132] Blumenthal (1979b) 396-397, in a brief discussion in fact reports Themistius as suggesting that the productive intellect "is a *theos* [god] other than the first." Certainly the commentator uses the epithet "divine" of this intellect (102.34), and refers to its thinking as "more divine" than discursive thinking (100.7); in both cases he is no doubt following *De Anima* 1.4, 408b29, part of a text that he cites and analyses at some length (cf. 101.19-23 in its context). Themistius, however, shows no signs of being inspired by Aristotelian statements (such as *Ethica Nicomachea* 10.7, 1177b26-1178a2) about the god-like character of a life of intellectual virtue.

[133] See notes 78 and 218 to the translation. The larger question of the relation between Themistius' account of this intellect and his interpretation of God's thinking in his commentary on *Metaphysics* 12 (*Lambda*) would merit further investigation. It has recently been opened up by Pines (1987) 186-187.

angle brackets that are left without comment are his emendations. Other changes to the text are recorded in the footnotes. Heinze's edition was based on only a limited investigation of the manuscript tradition. His text does, however, correspond fairly closely to that followed in William of Moerbeke's translation.[134] The Arabic version, by contrast, transmits a significantly different recension.[135] The changes introduced here in light of its readings[136] will reveal the limitations of Heinze's text. Further research on the Greek manuscript tradition might well lead to more extensive revisions. Equally, a closer understanding of Themistius' often highly elliptical style is needed to decide on whether or not in some cases the text is corrupt.[137]

This is the first translation of these passages into English. Parts of the paraphrase of *De Anima* 3.4 and 3.5 were translated into French in O. Ballériaux's thesis, and the whole paraphrase translated into Italian by V. De Falco. Both versions have been helpful, though they rely more heavily than I have thought necessary on terminology inherited from the medieval translation.

In a paraphrase such as Themistius' it is particularly difficult to identify variant readings in the quotations of Aristotelian texts. The difference between a quoted text and the standard Aristotelian text of modern critical editions may in some cases be the result of Themistius' access to a different source, but in others simply the product of paraphrase or casual quotation. It would have been cumbersome, and certainly irrelevant in this study, to deal in detail with this issue whenever it arose. It is, therefore,

---

[134] See Verbeke (1957) xciii. Of the manuscripts employed by Heinze it corresponds most closely to his Q (Laur. 87.25).

[135] See Lyons (1955), and the introduction to Lyons (1973) xiii-xiv. Lyons reports that there is a "totally different" Arabic version of the paraphrase of 3.3-4, 428b2-429b31 (that is, part of the material translated here). Since this version was not known to medieval and renaissance thinkers, a translation has not been sought for the purposes of the present study.

[136] These are all based on Browne's analysis and reconstruction of the Greek text.

[137] For some examples of this problem in the present translation see 105.5 (with note 133) and 112.33-34 (with note 208).

discussed only where it seemed indispensable to an understanding of Themistius' text.[138]

In the paraphrastic sections parts of the translation are correlated with the portions of the Aristotelian text they paraphrase, even if this occasionally disrupts the syntax of the original. This organization is, however, less easily imposed on the paraphrase of *De Anima* 3.5, and is inapplicable in the excursus. In these sections Aristotelian references have, therefore, been more frequently added within the translation. Elsewhere the reader with an Aristotelian text or translation to hand should readily detect brief quotations within paraphrases. Although no single English translation of the *De Anima* has been followed, the Greekless reader will probably find Hamlyn's version the most serviceable companion.

The notes to the translation deal primarily with the sources and intrinsic character of Themistius' exposition, and with its contribution to the history of the Aristotelian noetic. It would have been inappropriate in the context of the present study to comment at length on his other interpretations of Aristotelian texts.[139]

---

[138] It can be best pursued by perusing the apparatus criticus to Siwek's edition, though in some cases his evidence needs supplementing from Ross.

[139] For one example of such an exercise see Todd (1981).

The *De Intellectu*

Attributed to Alexander of Aphrodisias

Translated by
Frederic M. Schroeder

THE *DE INTELLECTU*

OUTLINE

<1. THE MATERIAL INTELLECT: 106.19-107.20>

106.19: Intellect, according to ARISTOTLE, is threefold. One type is material intellect, but by "material" I do not mean that it is a substrate like matter (for I call matter a substrate capable of becoming a particular thing through the presence of a form), but since what it is for matter to be matter lies in its capacity [to become] all things, then that in which this capacity and potentiality itself lies is, in so far as it is potential, material.

106.23: Indeed intellect, which is not yet thinking but is capable of becoming such is material and such a faculty of the soul is the material intellect, which although it is in actuality none of the things that exist, is capable of becoming all of them, if it is really possible for there to be acts of thought about everything that exists.

106.27: For what is destined to apprehend*[1] all things should not be in actuality any one of them in its own nature. For the intrusion of its own form** in the apprehension of things lying outside it would impede acts of thought about them.

106.30: For neither do the senses apprehend those things in which their being consists. For this reason therefore vision which is capable of apprehending colours has as colourless the organ in which it exists and through which apprehension [occurs] for it. For water is colourless in its own [*107*] colour. Furthermore, the sense of smell [arises] from air (and this is odourless) and is capable of apprehending odours. Touch too does not perceive things which are hot, or cold, or rough, or smooth in the same degree as itself, but things which vary from it in greater or lesser degree. And this is so since it would be impossible for touch, as

---

[1] Asterisks identify terms and expressions that are the subject of detailed discussion in the Commentary.

a body, not to possess these contrarieties; for every body that is natural and comes into existence is tangible.

107.5: To sum up then, *just as* in the case of the senses it is impossible for a sense which possesses some [quality] to be capable of apprehending and discerning [the quality] that it possesses, *so also* since intellect is an act of apprehending and discerning objects of thought, it is not at all possible for it to be [one] of the objects discerned by it.

107.8: It has the capacity for apprehending everything that exists, if it is really possible [for it] to think everything.* It is then none of the things that are in actuality, but it is potentially everything. For this is what it is for it to be intellect.

107.11: For the senses that operate through bodies are not [identical with] the [objects] they apprehend, but they are some other things in actuality, while the power [of perception] belongs to a particular body. For this reason it is through the body being affected in some way that the apprehension of objects of perception occurs. That is why not every sense can apprehend everything; for it is in itself already something in actuality.

107.15: But [material] intellect does not apprehend things that exist by means of body since it is neither a faculty of body, nor is it affected, nor is it one of the things that exist totally in actuality, nor is it that which is potential as a particular thing, but it is simply a capacity for a certain sort of entelechy and soul and a capacity of receiving forms and thoughts. This intellect, being material, exists in all beings that share in the complete soul,* that is, human beings.

<2. THE INTELLECT IN THE STATE OF POSSESSION: 107.21-28>

107.21: Different again is [the intellect] once it is engaged in thinking and is in a state of possessing thought and is capable of acquiring by its own capacity the forms of objects of thought.

107.22: It is analogous to men who are in the same state as craftsmen and are independently capable of creating the products relative to the craft. The first intellect, that is, was not like these men, but was more like those who are capable of taking up a craft and becoming craftsmen.

107.25: And the present intellect is the material intellect when once it has added a state of actively thinking. Such an intellect is present only* in those beings who are more complete, i.e., who *are* thinking. This then is the second intellect.

<3. THE PRODUCTIVE INTELLECT: 107.29-110.3>

107.29: The third intellect, on the other hand, in addition to the two already described, is the productive intellect through which the material intellect enters a state of possession, and this productive intellect is analogous, as ARISTOTLE says, to light. For *as* light becomes for colours that are potentially visible the cause of their becoming actually visible, *so also* does this third intellect make the potential and material intellect intellect in actuality by producing a state where thought is possessed.

107.34: This [productive intellect] is that which is in its own nature an object of thought and is such in actuality; [*108*] for it is productive of thinking and leads the material intellect into actuality. It is therefore itself intellect, for the immaterial form that alone is by its own nature an object of thought is intellect.

108.3: For the enmattered forms that are potentially objects of thought become such [i.e., in actuality] by means of the intellect. For intellect, by separating them from the matter with which they have their being, itself makes them actual objects of thought and then each of them, whenever it is thought of, becomes in actuality both an object of thought and intellect, although previously they were not such even in their own nature.

108.7: For intellect in actuality is nothing other than the form that is thought of; thus each of these too, though not just objects of thought simply, becomes intellect when it is thought. For *just as* knowledge in actuality is identical with the actual object of knowledge and *just as* perception in actuality is identical with the actual object of perception and the actual object of perception is identical with actual perception, *so also* is intellect in actuality identical with the actual object of thought and the actual object of thought identical with the actual intellect.

108.14: For intellect, by receiving the form of the object that is thought and separating it from matter, thus makes it an actual object of thought and becomes itself intellect in actuality. If indeed there is something that exists that is an actual object of thought in its own nature and [if] what can be such is [so] from itself by being immaterial, not from the intellect that separates it from matter, then such a thing is perpetually intellect in actuality. For intellect is that which is the actual object of thought.

108.19: Indeed this both is the object of thought by its own nature and is intellect in actuality, and it becomes the cause of the material intellect's separating, imitating and thinking with reference to such a form and of its also making each of the enmattered forms itself an object of thought. It is the productive intellect that is called [intellect] from without,* not because it is a part and a faculty of our soul, but because it comes to exist in us from outside whenever we think of it (if thinking indeed occurs through the reception of form), and it is itself an immaterial form in that, when thought of, it is never accompanied by matter, nor is it being separated from matter.

108.26: Since it has this character, it is reasonable that it be separate from us since what it is to be intellect does not lie in its being thought by *us,* but it has this character by its own nature, as it is in actuality both intellect and object of thought. Such a form and essence that is separate from matter is imperishable.

108.29: For this reason too the productive intellect, because it is such a form by virtue of being from without in actuality, is reasonably called *immortal** intellect by ARISTOTLE [*109*].

109.1: Now each of the other forms that are thought is also intellect when it is thought, but is not intellect from without or from outside, but what becomes [such] when it is thought. But since this intellect exists even before it is thought, it is reasonable that when it is thought it both be and be said [to be] from without.

109.4: The intellect that is in a state of possessing [thoughts] can, when active, think itself, not in so far as it is intellect (for then thinking and being thought will exist for it simultaneously and in the same respect), but in fact just in so far as the actual intellect is identical with the actual objects of thought.

109.7: Indeed when it thinks these objects it thinks itself, if, that is, the things that it thinks become intellect when they are thought. For if the actual intellect is [in actuality] the things that are thought and it does think them, then it comes to think itself. For when it is thinking it becomes identical with the objects of thought, but when not thinking it is different from them.

109.11: So also perception can be said to perceive itself when it perceives the objects that become in actuality identical with it; for, as we have said, perception in actuality is also the object of perception. Indeed perception and intellect, through the reception of forms apart from matter, apprehend objects that are proper to them.

109.14: Furthermore intellect could be said to think itself not in so far as it is intellect, but in so far as it is itself also an object of thought; for it will apprehend [itself] as an object of thought (just as it also apprehends each of the other objects of thought) and not as intellect.

109.17: Being also an object of thought is an accidental property of intellect, for since it is itself also something that exists and is not an object of perception, there remains for it [only] to be an object of thought.* For if it were *qua* intellect and in so far as it is intellect that it were thought by itself, it would not think anything except what is intellect. As a result, it would think itself exclusively. But since it thinks objects of thought that are not intellect prior to being thought, then it thinks itself as this type of thing, i.e., as one of the objects of thought.

109.22: It follows that when this intellect advances from the material intellect it comes to think itself accidentally. And in about the same way the first [material] intellect [thinks itself] and the actual intellect thinks itself and for the same reason. But the latter has an advantage over the former, for it does not think anything other than itself. For by being an object of thought it is thought by itself and by being an object of thought in actuality and by its own nature it will always be the object of thinking, obviously by the agency of that which is thinking in actuality <perpetually>.

109.27: Since it thinks in actuality perpetually, it is itself exclusively intellect; it will therefore always be thinking itself. And exclusively [itself] in so far as it is simple;* for intellect that is simple thinks a simple object and there is no other simple object of thought than itself. For this [intellect] is *unmixed* and immaterial and has nothing in itself in potentiality. It will therefore think itself exclusively.

109.31: Thus in so far as it is intellect it will think itself as an object of thought, [*110*] but in so far as it is in actuality both intellect and object of thought, it will think itself perpetually, while in so far as it is simple it will think only itself. For by being itself the only thing that is simple, it has the capacity to think a simple object, and it is itself the only object of thought that is simple.

<4. ARISTOTLE ON THE INTELLECT FROM WITHOUT: 110.4-112.5>

110.4: I heard* <the> [views] on the intellect from without from [*sc.* derived from] ARISTOTLE and I have retained them for myself.**

110.5: The [considerations] that moved ARISTOTLE to introduce the intellect from without* were said to be the following:* the

analogy with objects of perception and the analogy with all things
that come into existence.

110.7: For *just as* with all things that come into existence there
is something that is passive and also something that is productive
and thirdly something that comes into existence from these (and
similarly in the case of objects of perception; for the organ of
sense is passive, the object of perception is productive and that
which comes into existence is apprehension of the object of
perception by means of the organ of sense), *in just the same way*
in the case of the intellect too he maintained that there must be
a productive intellect that can bring the potential and material
intellect into activity (its activity being to make all that exists
objects of thought for itself).

110.13: For as the objects of perception make perception active
and actual, so there must be certain objects of thought that make
intellect also actual, being themselves objects of thought. For
nothing can produce an effect on something unless it is itself in
actuality.

110.16: None of the things thought by *us* is in actuality an object
of thought. For *our* intellect thinks the objects of perception that
are potentially objects of thought. These, in turn, become objects
of thought by the agency of the intellect. This then is the activity
of the intellect, to separate and abstract by its own power objects
of perception that are such in actuality from the things in
company with which they are objects of perception and to define
them as they are in themselves.

110.20: If this is indeed the activity of the intellect that previously existed in potentiality and if it is necessary that that which
comes into existence, i.e. is brought from potentiality into actuality does so by the agency of something existing in actuality,
then there must also be a productive intellect existing in actuality
which will make the intellect that until then is potential capable
of being active, i.e. of thinking. The intellect [that enters from
without] has this character. These then were the [considerations]

that moved him [*sc.* ARISTOTLE] to introduce the intellect from without.

110.25: There will then be something that is indeed an actual object of thought, being such by its own nature, as again there is also an object of perception that does not become such through the [act of perception]. This [object of thought] is the intellect [from without], a nature and an essence, not to be known by anything other than the intellect. For it is *not* an object of perception at least, nor do all the objects of thought become so through our intellect, even though they are not objects of thought in their own nature. Instead there is something that is indeed in itself an object of thought, being such by its own nature. It is *this* very object that the potential intellect thinks when it is being brought to completion i.e. is [in the course of] maturing.

110.31: For *just as* the capacity for walking which man has as soon as he comes into existence is brought into actuality as time advances, with the man not being brought to completion through being affected in some way, *in the same manner [111]* the intellect also thinks the natural objects of thought when it has been brought to completion and makes objects of perception its objects of thought in as much as it has the capacity to produce this effect. For intellect is not in its own nature passive so as to come into being and be affected by a different thing as is perception. Quite the contrary.

111.4: For while perception occurs through an affection, since it is something passive and apprehension for it involves being affected, intellect is productive. For it can think most things and at the same time becomes their creator [producer] in order to think them, unless someone wanted to claim in this regard that intellect too was passive in so far as it is receptive of the forms. Receiving does after all seem to be a case of being affected.

111.8: Now intellect certainly does have this [i.e., passivity] in common with perception, but since each of them is characterized and defined not by that which it has in common with something else but from its characteristic property, then what [intellect] has in common with perception would be characterized by its characteristic property; thus if the receptivity of forms is common to it and perception, even if not in the same way, and yet its characteristic property is being productive of the forms that it receives, it would *a fortiori* be characterized on the basis of its productivity. Thus intellect is active, not passive.

111.15: Furthermore, to produce is prior for it [to being affected] and is its essence. For it first produces an object of thought by abstraction, then in this way receives one of the things that it thinks and defines it as some particular thing. For even if it separates and receives [form] at the same time, still the separation is the prior act of thought. For this is what it is for it to be receptive of form.

111.19: *Just as* we say that fire is most productive in that it consumes all the matter it receives and so provides nutriment for itself (indeed it is affected in so far as it is nourished), *in the same manner* the intellect which is in us must also be considered to be productive. For it itself makes objects of thought of things that are not in actuality objects of thought. For nothing else is an object of thought except the intellect that exists in actuality and in itself.

111.23: And the things that become objects of thought through something that thinks, as well as the latter's activities, are also themselves intellect when they are thought. Thus if there were not intellect there would be no object of thought; for in that case there would neither be a natural intellect (for it itself is the only thing of this sort), nor would there be any result of its agency. For if it did not exist it would not be productive.

111.27: That which is intellect by nature and from without becomes co-operative with the intellect that is in us, since the other objects of thought would not even exist in potentiality unless there were an object of thought existing in its own nature [i.e., independently]. Since it is indeed an object of thought in its own nature when through being thought it has come to exist as intellect in the thinker and is thought from without, it is immortal and instills in the material intellect the state of possession that results in its thinking the potential objects of thought.

111.32: For *just as* light, being productive of actual vision, is itself seen along with its concomitants [*sc.* illumined things] and it is through it that colour [is visible], *so also* the intellect from without becomes the cause of thinking for us, when it is itself thought [by us], not by producing intellect itself but by, through its own nature, completing the intellect that exists and bringing it to its proper [activities].

111.36: Thus intellect is by its nature an object of thought, while the other objects of thought exist by its craft [*112*] and are its productions which the potential [intellect] produces, not by being affected, i.e., coming into existence through something else (for it was after all intellect even before it became active), but by maturing and coming to completion. When it is completed it thinks what are by their nature objects of thought and those that depend upon its proper activity and craft. For productivity is proper to the intellect and for it thinking is being active, not being affected.

<5. THE INTELLECT IMMANENT IN THE PHYSICAL WORLD:
112.5-113.12>

112.5: Wishing to show that the intellect was immortal and to escape the problems that they raise for the intellect from without, *viz.* that it must change place and cannot, if it is indeed incorporeal, either be in place or change place and be in different places at different times, according to his own reflection, he said the following concerning the intellect that is said to exist in the whole of the mortal body.

112.9: He claimed that the intellect is both in matter as a substance in a substance* and that it exists in actuality by realizing its own activities perpetually. So whenever from a body that is the result of a blend fire or something like it emerges from the mixture** with the result that it can also provide an instrument to this intellect that is present in this mixture (because intellect is [*ex hypothesi*] in the whole of body and this too [i.e., the mixture] is body) this instrument is called the potential intellect, a suitable potentiality that supervenes upon such a mixture of bodies for the purpose of receiving the actual intellect.

112.16: Whenever [the actual intellect] acquires this instrument, it at that point acts, as it were, instrumentally and with reference to its matter and by means of matter and it is then that *we* are said to think. For our intellect is composed of the potentiality that is the instrument of the divine intellect (what ARISTOTLE calls the potential intellect) and of the divine intellect's activity. If neither of these is present, it is impossible for us to think.

112.21: Right from the first deposit of sperm the intellect in actuality is what pervades everything and exists in actuality, as also in the case of any other body at all. Whenever it is also active through our potentiality then this is called *our* intellect and it is *we* who think, as if one were to imagine a craftsman at one time active in his craft without instruments, but at another with instruments too, where his activity with respect to the craft is directed towards matter. In the same manner also the divine intellect is perpetually acting (that is why it also exists in actuality) and yet so instrumentally, whenever such an instrument comes into existence from the combination of bodies and their temperate blend. This intellect at that point engages in an act that indeed is of a material kind and this is our intellect.

112.31: Indeed it is separated [from the instrumental intellect] in the same manner in which it is introduced. It is not the case that it changes its place by being somewhere else but that by being everywhere it remains even in the body dissolved by the separation [*113*] [of its constituents] where the instrumental factor [*to organikon* = that capable of an instrumental role] is destroyed; similarly the craftsman, after he has discarded his instruments, is even then active, but not in a material and instrumental activity. Indeed he said that if we must really assume that according to

ARISTOTLE the intellect is divine and immortal, we must think of it in this way and not otherwise.

113.4: And he said that the *text* in the third book of the *De Anima* should be co-ordinated with these doctrines and that the *positive state* (*hexis*) and the *light* (430a15) should be referred to the intellect that is everywhere.

113.6: Now this intellect *either* administers things here all by itself and combines and separates them with respect to their relation to the divine bodies, so that it is itself also the demiurge of [i.e., that which produces] the potential intellect, *or* it does this in concert with the well-ordered motion of the heavenly bodies. It is after all through the agency of the latter [motion] that things here come into existence, especially through the approach and departure of the sun, since they *either* come to be through the action of the latter and the intellect here, *or else* nature comes to be through these things [*sc.* heavenly bodies] and their motion, while nature itself administers individual things [*sc.* here] in concert with the intellect.

<6. CRITICISM OF THE ABOVE THEORY
OF THE IMMANENCE OF INTELLECT: 113.12-24>

113.12: It seemed right to me to resist these [doctrines], i.e., (1) that the intellect, though divine, is present in even the basest things, as the Stoics held; and (2) that there is an intellect and guiding providence present generally even in things here (and indeed that providence occurs through the relation of things here to the divine bodies); and (3) that thinking is not dependent on us nor is this even our function, but that from the moment of our coming into existence there is inherent in us by nature both the combination of the potential and instrumental intellect and the activity brought about by the intellect from without.

113.18: Now that which comes into existence in someone by being thought does not change place; for neither do the forms of objects of perception when we perceive them come into existence in the organs of sense as their places. But the intellect from without is said to be separate and is separated from us, not by, as it were, going away somewhere and changing place, but *while* separate in the sense that it is independent and not accompanied by matter, it is separated from us by not being thought, *not* by going away elsewhere. For that is how it came to be in us too.

Commentary

106.19: The first sentence is very revealing for the character of the *De Intellectu.* Clearly, the threefold intellect has been arrived at by some antecedent process of reasoning; here we are presented rather abruptly with its results, together with some of the reasons for advancing them. The very use of ordinal numerals gives the impression of notes rather than of careful philosophical composition, as in Alexander's *De Anima.*

In the *De Anima* of Alexander we are presented, not so much with three intellects, as with an account of the phases of intellectual development. Stabile 57 correctly contrasts the present work in remarking that: "In the *De Intellectu* Alexander describes the aspects of intellect, not from the point of view of this development, but as aspects of the intellective power of man." Aristotle *De Anima* 3.5, 430a10-14, of course, speaks of active and of potential and (by analogy with the rest of nature) material aspects of intellect. On the question of the materialism mistakenly attributed both to the *De Anima* and the *De Intellectu,* see Introduction pp. 7-13.

106.27: This is the first argument for the view that the material intellect must be none of the objects of thought (cf. Aristotle *De Anima* 2.4, 415a16-20; 3.4, 429a13-18).

*The verb here translated as "apprehend" (*antilambanesthai* [106.27]) is not Aristotelian. Alexander uses *antilêpsis* (the noun) of sensation generally (*De Anima* 60.2; 53.30-34; *In Topica* [CAG 2.2] 343.11) where Aristotle would use *krinein* ("to judge, discern"); cf. Todd (1974) 209. This word and others from the same root can have the sense, not of passive reception, but of active "seizing"; cf. Moraux (1942) 71 and Stabile 137.

** "The intrusion (*paremphainomenon* [*106.28*]) of its own form," cf. Aristotle *De Anima* 3.4, 429a20.

106.30: The analogy of the senses introduces the second argument (extending to 107.8) why the material intellect must not be itself informed. Thus sight does not perceive colour, i.e., it is not informed with respect to what it perceives. Similarly smell is odourless and touch cannot perceive that which possesses its own degree of roughness or smoothness. The analogy to sight is from Aristotle *De Anima* 2.7, 418b26-27; the analogy with touch is from 2.11, 424a1-10. See also Aristotle's more general analogy of perception and thought at 3.4, 429a16-18.

107.8: * "to think everything" (107.9), cf. Aristotle *De Anima* 3.4, 429a18; cf. 3.4, 429b30-31.

107.21: Here the state (*hexis*) of possessing thought (the *habitus* of the medieval translations) is introduced. Aristotle *De Anima* 3.5, 430a15 describes the productive intellect as a *hexis* (state) and then as an *energeia* (activity) (3.5, 430a18). Ross (1961) 296 takes this as a sign that the passage is "carelessly written." The author of the *De Intellectu* distinguishes these as different phases of intellect—i.e., the state (*hexis*) of possessing thought is the perfection of the material intellect. The word "activity" (*energeia*) in the Aristotelian text is attached to the productive intellect.

In the *De Intellectu* the intellect in the state of possession has the power of abstraction that in the *De Anima* of Alexander is confined to the material intellect (Moraux [1942] 157; Stabile 155). Discrepancies may be explained from the fact that in the *De Intellectu* "Alexander does not deal with the development of the *nous hulikos* [material intellect]; the function of the intelligibles as the agent cause of the actualization of the intellect is virtually non-existent" (Stabile 157).

107.22: In the reference to "craftsmen" there is doubtless a dependence on the distinction between potential and actual knowledge at Aristotle *De Anima* 3.4, 429b5-9; cf. 2.5,

417a22-417b2 and Themistius *In De Anima* 3.4, 95.9-16. We may see a distinction between the material intellect as first entelechy and the intellect in the state of posssession as second entelechy. For the distinction between first and second entelechy see Aristotle *De Anima* 2.1, 412a21-28. See Schroeder (1982) 120 and Introduction pp. 8-12 for the view that in Alexander's *De Anima* the material intellect is as *dunamis* to be understood as the equivalent of an Aristotelian first entelechy awaiting completion.

107.25: *"only" (*êdê* [107.28]). In the word index at Alexander's *De Anima* and the *De Anima Mantissa* in SA 2.1:205, Bruns lists the following as instances of *êdê* in the sense *a temporali ad logicum usum translatum* : 107.15; 21; 26 (the present occurrence); 27; 112.30, a sense which is not to be found in LSJ. The present translation attempts carefully to allow for the context of each occurrence. The text at 107.26 may be compared with Alexander *De Anima* 74.6 where *êdê* means "just" [or "only"] among the more complete [beings]" in contrast with the molluscs of the preceding clause; cf. Alexander *De Anima* 35.21-22.

107.29: For an account of illuminationist doctrine, see on 108.19 below. The analogy is incomplete. The productive intellect as supreme form, object of thought, free of material substrate serves as the primal object of intellective vision for the potential intellect and it is with reference to this that it abstracts forms as objects of thought from matter. The action of the productive intellect is therefore not directly upon the forms or objects of thought as the action of light is exerted upon visible objects. Instead it acts directly upon the material intellect in conferring the intellect in the state of possession.

107.34: This passage contains an important principle that at first sight offers some difficulty to the student of the *De Intellectu* (and to the student of the Alexandrian noetic generally). The productive intellect is said to be itself object of thought. Indeed it is not in its role as intellect, but in its capacity as object of thought that it contributes to the genesis of human intellection. Here in the *De*

Intellectu it serves as the primary object of thought for the material intellect and thereby confers on the material intellect the intellect in the state of possession (see on 108.19 below). We might then expect that the author would be arguing the case that the productive intellect is also object of thought. He instead assumes as a premiss its character as object of thought, and then argues that it is also intellect. But that which is supremely object of thought cannot be so only because it is addressed by our minds. (This link in the argument may be supplied from 108.25-26.) Therefore it must be addressed by a supreme intellect that will be identical with itself.

108.3: The author here elaborates the Aristotelian doctrine that intellect and object of thought are one. This occurs at Aristotle *De Anima* 3.5, 430a19-20 and at 3.7, 431a1-2. Ross (1961) 296 deletes it from the former passage, but retains it in the latter, on the grounds that "they are harmless in ch. 7, which is in any case a collection of scraps; here they seriously interfere with the course of thought, which without these would be continuous." Ross (1961) 303 observes that, according to Ps.-Philoponus *In De Anima* (CAG 15) 558.4-6, Alexander obelized the passage at 431a1-3. It may be that the *De Intellectu*, as it is a reflection on Aristotle *De Anima* 3.5, reads this passage in that chapter. It is certainly convenient to the noetic which is offered here to do so. Themistius, however, paraphrases 430a19-21 from 3.5, but ignores it for 3.7 (see Themistius' paraphrase on 3.7 below and note 203). The same general point (that intellect and object of thought are one) occurs at Aristotle *De Anima* 3.4, 430a1-2. If we accept Owens' resistance to Bywater's emendation and read δὲ αὐτὸν for Bywater's δι' αὐτοῦ at Aristotle *De Anima* 3.4, 429b9, we may see here a reference to that passage (so understood by Alexander at *De Anima* 86.14-29; see Owens 107).

108.14: The distinction between classes of forms as objects of thought is doubtless dependent upon Aristotle *De Anima* 3.5, 430a3-9 (see also below note 37 to the translation of Themistius). Merlan (1963) 16-17; (1967) 119-120; (1970) 118

establishes that there are two classes of forms, objects of thought
(see *De Anima* 87.24-88.3; 89.13-15; 90.2-11), which he describes as immanent and transcendent intelligibles (*enula/aüla,*
"enmattered/immaterial" or *phusei noêta,* "objects of thought by
nature"). The enmattered or immanent forms, i.e., objects of
thought, exist only in the moment they are thought. The same is
true in principle of the immaterial or transcendent forms, objects
of thought, but these, as they are always objects of the thought of
the productive (transcendent) intellect, are always in existence.
Donini (1974) 32-34 sees in Alexander *De Anima* 88-89 an
apparent conflict between the notion that the productive intellect
is one and yet its objects of thought are many. He argues for the
identity of the productive intellect with the forms, objects of
thought and sees in this a source for Plotinus 5.1 [10].9. He
denies, however, that the dichotomy of the two classes of forms,
objects of thought exists in the *De Intellectu,* where there is but
one productive intellect that is also supreme form, object of
thought and then a plurality of immanent forms, objects of
thought. Donini (1974) 60 compares *De Intellectu* 108.16-22
and Alexander *De Anima* 87.25-29.

Moraux (1978b) 532-533, in a review of Donini (1974),
argues for a plurality of immaterial, transcendent forms, objects
of thought in the *De Intellectu* (see 110.13-15; 111.1; 112.3).
Moraux also observes that at Alexander *De Anima* 87.24-29 we
encounter the same doctrine in the context of establishing the
identity of the immaterial forms or objects of thought and
productive intellect (singular). Thus in both works singular and
plural must for this purpose be interchangeable. Sharples (1987)
1211 note 125 draws our attention to an apparent statement of
the plurality of immaterial, transcendent forms, i.e., objects of
thought in fr. VI from Appendix III to Moraux (1942) 213, now
in a revised text in Verbeke (1966) 82.13-24. Sharples (1987)
1211 argues that the discussion of such pure forms in *De Anima*
87.24-88.16 precedes discussion of the productive intellect and
is not so much an argument for plurality as an introduction to the
notion of transcendent, immaterial forms, objects of thought. It

seems indifferent whether such form is, in this passage, referred to in the singular or in the plural. He refers us to *De Anima* 87.25-28 (cf. *De Intellectu* 108.16-19) for the hypothetical nature of this discussion. In subsequent passages, where the productive intellect is the theme of discussion, references are generally in the singular (the one plural reference at *De Anima* 90.11ff. "seems to be a generalization").

The notion that there is one class of objects of thought corresponding to the Platonic Forms and another corresponding to enmattered forms is to be found in Alcinous *Didaskalikos* p. 155 Hermann. (On the disputed question of the authorship of this treatise, often ascribed to Albinus, see the literature cited at Donini [1982] 103 with notes 14 and 15.) See also Merlan (1963) 68; Merlan (1967) 117 claims that "[Alexander] insisted that only the singular existed in the proper sense of the word and thus treated the transcendent intelligibles as individuals (and, with Aristotle, rejected ideas, precisely because he took them to be universals)." See, however, Moraux (1978b) 532-533 who insists upon Alexander's claim to Aristotelian orthodoxy in positing separate forms, i.e., objects of thought.

108.19: The productive intellect is considered here, not in its capacity as intellect, but as supreme object of thought (cf. 107.34). It is by being an immaterial object of thought and form, existing independently of our thought, that it may serve as the primary object of thought. It is with reference to this primary object of intellective vision that the human intellect is capable of abstracting forms as objects of thought from matter. The productive intellect is accordingly said to impart to the material intellect the state of thinking objects of thought that are in potentiality (111.27). The human intellect is said to imitate (108.21) the productive intellect, doubtless in producing the objects of thought it abstracts from matter. This notion of imitation has a distinctly Platonic ring. We may well ask whether this primal vision is a sort of antenatal Platonic *anamnêsis*. It is said to be seen together with its concomitants, like light (111.32). This suggests that, although the address to the productive intellect as supreme object of thought is logically prior to the abstraction and recognition of the enmattered forms as objects of thought, it may be temporally simultaneous.

The doctrine presented here differs radically from that of Alexander's *De Anima*. In the Alexandrian theory of light, the source of light is supremely luminous and is also thereby cause of illumination. On the other hand, illumination is not merely an effect of the source. It is a joint effect produced when both *illuminans* and *illuminatum* are juxtaposed. The *illuminatum* makes its own contribution to the effect produced within this pattern of causation (*De Anima* 42.19-43.11). By analogy, the productive intellect as supreme object of thought is the cause for enmattered forms of their becoming objects of thought. Yet when the enmattered forms are juxtaposed with the productive intellect, they make their own contribution to the effect produced (88.26-89.6). That juxtaposition takes place when the human intellect has evolved to the point of being able to abstract the enmattered forms from their substrate (see Schroeder [1981] and Introduction pp. 13-19). There is no suggestion, as here, that the productive intellect (as object of thought) serves for the human intellect as a prior object of intellective vision by reference to which the human intellect is enabled to advance from the material intellect to the intellect in the state of possession.

Moraux (1984) 414 appeals to 111.22-33 to support the view that the productive intellect *qua* object of thought is the cause for enmattered forms of their becoming objects of thought. It is difficult to see such a doctrine in this text. On the relation of this material to the question of authorship see Introduction pp. 6-20.

*"from without" (108.23). The phrase *nous thurathen*, "intellect from without" occurs twice in the *De Generatione Animalium* of Aristotle, at 2.3, 736b13-20 and at 2.6, 744b22. The first of these passages does not invite the sort of speculation put forth in the *De Intellectu* or elsewhere in late Greek Aristotelian commentary. Moraux (1955) discusses this passage, which is in fact a crux, with reference to its biological content in the *De Generatione Animalium* and shows that it is an aporetic reflection on

embryology. He expels the intellect from without from the second passage through textual emendation.

For Alexander the intellect from without is independent of human thought (*De Anima* 90.21-23). It is not a faculty of the human soul, but a divine element present in man (90.23-91.6). In other words, it is equated with the productive intellect. Here in the *De Intellectu* it is explicitly equated with the productive intellect and its immaterial character is stressed. For a recent discussion of the intellect from without from the end of the first century BC, see Moraux (1984) 407-410.

108.29: *"immortal" (108.30). The reference is to Aristotle *De Anima* 3.5, 430a23. Alexander *De Anima* 90.14-16 denies the immortality both of the potential intellect and the intellect in the state of possession. Alexander bases his theory of immortality on the identity of mind and object of thought in Aristotle *De Anima* 3.4, 430a3-4; 3.5, 430a19-20; *Metaphysics* 12.7, 1072b21. The objects of thought abstracted by the human mind from their material substrate are, since they have no objective existence apart from being thought, perishable (Alexander *De Anima* 88.14-15; 90.2-11; 90.24-91.4).

Yet if the object of thought is of itself intelligible in act, it is also by nature imperishable. The intellect that thinks such an object becomes like it (*De Anima* 87.25-88.10) and is thus rendered immortal (89.21-90.2). Alexander speaks (90.13-17) of an intellect that becomes immortal when it has thought the supreme object of thought. It is difficult to reconcile the description of this intellect with the denial (90.14-16) of the immortality of the potential intellect and of intellect in the state of possession.

Our perplexity is only increased by the statement that, while the intellect from without is immortal, the potential intellect and its perfection, the intellect in the state of possession that thinks the intellect from without as object of thought, in addition to its other objects of thought, is mortal (90.23-91.5). And this is asserted despite the fact that the intellect from without is said to come about "in us" (90.23-91.1).

This immortal facet of human personality could only be the concept of divinity we have formed by knowing it (Moraux [1942] 97-98). The intellect in the state of possession is said (88.5-6) to become the (immortal) object of thought when it thinks it. We might then be tempted to believe that, after all, the intellect in the state of possession must be immortal. It must be remembered, however, that the intellect in the state of possession is the capacity for thinking at will rather than actual thought (85-86).

Davidson 130 remarks: "Alexander accordingly may be taken as saying that no part of any human faculty is immortal, but when the intellect *in habitu* has an actual thought of an indestructible form that thought alone remains immortal. The immortal actual thought in man, Alexander concludes, is 'the intellect generated in us from without (90.19).' That is to say, the actual thought of an indestructible form does not exist independently—*qua* intelligible object—but only as identical with the form which is the object of thought. Thus hardly anything human and surely nothing individual can be said to characterize the human thoughts Alexander considered to be immortal."

A simpler way of looking at it is provided by Stabile 188: "Human immortality is really nothing more than the presence of the *nous thurathen* [intellect from without] in man." Sharples (1987) 1204 now remarks: "Indeed for Alexander our intellect is nothing in itself, but becomes identical with its objects; accordingly, when it apprehends the pure and imperishable form of the divine intellect it becomes identical with that form, but this seems to show us no more than the immortality of the concept of the intellect in us."

It is not necessary to interpret the word "immortal" in the present passage as referring to any form of human intellect. Whether we would in principle wish to elucidate the question of immortality in the *De Intellectu* from the *De Anima* of Alexander would depend on the position taken with respect to the question of authorship (see Introduction pp. 6-22). At *De Intellectu* 111.27 the productive intellect is said to serve as a form free of a material substrate; as such it is the primary object addressed by the human mind which, with reference to it, may recognize and abstract enmattered forms. Davidson 130 remarks, "an indestructible actual human thought would already exist at that early point." There is, however, no development of this idea in the *De Intellectu,* nor would this compel us to conclude that anything but the actual thought (and that precariously) of this form is in any sense immortal.

In the section from 112.5 on, the author's opponent says that the productive intellect survives man and, as it is omnipresent, "remains even in the body dissolved by the separation [of its constituents]" (112.32-113.1). This, however, is scarcely a description of personal immortality. The productive intellect is ours when it employs our intellectual equipment as its instrument (112.21). When we die, these instruments are abandoned (112.31). In any case this section may be a fragment from another work distinct from the material which we are discussing (see Introduction pp. 22-31). The Arabic translation of *nous thurathen* ("intellect from without") as "acquired intellect" suggests something which is human and opens the way to the immortality of a human faculty (Davidson 130). See also Thillet (1981) 17-24 who argues correctly that any sort of human immortality would arise only by implication.

109.17: * "there remains for it [only] to be an object of thought" (109.18). The notion is that the only remaining alternative is for it to be an object of thought.

109.27: * "simple" (*haplous* [109.28]; instances from lines 28-30). This word does not occur in the noetic section of Alexander *De Anima.* Perhaps this fact may serve as a further reason for our not seeing the *De Intellectu* as a work of Alexander.

110.4: * "I heard ... from Aristotle." This translation arises from an emendation: ⟨τὰ⟩ παρὰ 'Αριστοτέλους for παρὰ 'Αριστοτέλους. See the discussion of this crux in Introduction pp.22-31.

** "I have retained for myself" (110.4). The verb used here is *diasôzesthai.* Trabucco 119 refers us to Plato *Republic* 329a3 where the active voice of the verb is used of a proverb and translates "to keep in mind." This understanding of the verb would support the view (see Introduction pp. 22-25) that the reference is to contemporary, oral instruction. Note, however, the middle voice of the verb. In LSJ this use is glossed: "To save for oneself, preserve for oneself, retain." The reflexive force of the middle voice would point to a set of notes that the author has compiled for his own use. Themistius *In Analytica Posteriora* (CAG 5.1) 6.27 uses the active form of the verb in the sense "to get it right."

110.5: ***"were said to be the following" (110.5-6); cf. 110.24-25 (end of the section marked 110.5). As remarked in the Introduction p. 23, a pupil in late antiquity tended to be forward in advancing his personal claims to inside knowledge of his master and his background (for example, Porphyry *Vita Plotini* 13.10-17 and 15.1-6). This may explain his frequent and self-conscious resort to the personal pronoun to establish his intimate acquaintance with his teacher. (*Vita Plotini* 4.1-2; 8; 12; 5.60; 7.50; 11.11-12; 13.10; 15.11-12; 16.14; 17.12; 18.9; 21.21.; 23.12). For classical examples we may look to Xenophon's advertisement of his first-hand experience of Socratic dialogue (*Memorabilia* 1.3.8-13; 1.4.2; 2.4.1; 2.5.1; 4.3.2). This consideration should work against our seeing at reference to a contemporary teacher at 110.4; cf. Schroeder (1987) 518.

110.25: Here, as at 107.34 and 108.15, the productive intellect or intellect from without is said to be *per se* an object of thought by its own nature. We are told that it is this intellect from without *qua* object of thought that the potential intellect thinks in the course of being increased and completed. Now at 109.19 it is stated that it is with reference to the productive intellect *qua* object of thought that the material intellect extracts forms as objects of thought. It enters us from without whenever we think it. We may ask, when do we think the productive intellect/ intellect from without *qua* object of thought? Is it, for example, an object of thought for us at the moment of conception?

At 112.21 the source whom the author (112.5-113.24) is criticizing teaches that it is present right from the deposit of the sperm. The author dismisses this view at 113.12. Of course, if we adopt the view (see Introduction pp. 22-31) that the material from 112.5 to the end is independent and appended by a slipshod compiler, then it may not be legitimate to interpret the present passage in the light of earlier passages preceding 112.5-113.24.

The present text suggests rather that the intellect from without *qua* object of thought is an object of thought for the material intellect in the course of its natural development. The analogy with light as it is drawn at 111.32 (see Commentary *ad loc.*) tends to confirm this view. See also below on the analogy of walking at 110.31.

110.31: It may be of value to undertake a comparison with the use of the analogy of walking to intellectual development drawn by Alexander *De Anima* 82.5-15. There Alexander argues that the ability to walk exists in man by nature and will of itself progress toward its completion. The human mind will of itself progress toward the grasp of the universal and the knowledge that arises from synthesis. Yet the intellect in the state of possession and the accomplished act of thought are acquired and belong to the sage alone (cf. Themistius *In Analytica Posteriora* 65.21-66.3 for the analogy of the growth of intellect to walking; this may have been a scholastic commonplace).

At first sight, the statement at 110.32 would not seem to contradict the analogy at Alexander *De Anima* 82.5-15. The intellect proceeds by nature to the point at which it may abstract forms as objects of thought from objects of perception. Yet immediately above (110.25) the intellect is said to address the intellect from without as object of thought as it is completed and increased (*sc.* by nature). Since the analogy at 110.31 is meant to illustrate this statement, it must seem to present (however elliptically) doctrine contrary to that found in Alexander *De Anima* 82.5-15, that is, that the completion of the human intellect is not achieved by nature.

There remains another problem. The doctrine of 110.25 and 110.31 is in apparent conflict with statements at 111.27. There it is said that it is by being an object of thought in its own nature that the intellect from without, on entering us, imparts to us the intellect in the state of possession. Does this mean that the intellect from without is an object of thought for the human intellect before its increase and completion? An answer may be provided if we look again to Alexander *De Anima*. At *De Anima* 82.5-10, Alexander says that the intellect may progress by nature to the grasp of the universal, but not to intellect in the state of possession or to the accomplished act of thought. Here the progress to the intellect in the state of possession is natural and involves the address to the productive intellect *qua* object of thought. For Alexander the productive intellect is an object only for the human mind upon its completion (*De Anima* 84.22-24; 87.29-88.10; 89.21-91.6). Cf. Schroeder (1981) 224-225. The passages at 110.25 and 110.31 must mean that the human intellect already beholds the intellect from without as object as it becomes intellect in the state of possession; that it advances to that vision by nature; and that it is by that vision enabled to function as intellect in the state of possession.

111.32: The analogy of the intellect from without to light offered in the present passage is much more satisfactory than the elliptical analogy with light at 107.29 and 107.31. There it is said that as light renders potentially visible colours actually visible, so does the productive intellect make the potential and material intellect to be in act by imparting to it the intellect in the state of possession. The visibility of objects of perception is not, as we would expect, compared with the intelligibility of objects of thought, but with thinking.

Yet while the analogy is clearer, it is still elliptical: light (by being supremely visible?) is said to produce vision; by analogy, the intellect from without (by being supreme object of thought?) produces thought in us. It is also said that light produces the visibility of colour. Now the intellect from without does not produce the objects of thought directly. Rather, it enables the potential intellect to produce these. At 111.2 and 111.8, intellect is, as active, contrasted with sensation, as passive. Light will not, therefore, enable vision to produce visibles in the same way as the intellect from without enables the potential intellect to produce objects of thought.

The analogy of the productive intellect to light functions in a very different and more consistent manner at Alexander *De Anima* 88.26-89.6. There the productive intellect *qua* supreme object of thought produces the intelligibility of the objects of thought, even as light *qua* supremely visible produces the visibility of the visible objects. For a fuller treatment of this subject and for the notion that the objects of thought make their own contribution to intelligibility even as the *illuminata* make ther own contribution to illumination, see Schroeder (1981) and Introduction pp. 14-19.

Light is said here (111.33) to be itself seen along with its concomitants [illuminated things]. Earlier in this commentary (at 110.25 and 110.31) we raised the question of the point at which the intellect from without becomes an object of thought for the human intellect. It was suggested that the intellect from without is in some sense an object of thought for the human intellect throughout the course of its development, i.e., while it is being completed and increased and is in that way the cause of its development. Now when we see visible objects, we see at the same time the light by which they are illuminated. The vision of light and of the visibles may then be distinguished as two aspects of a single event, without implying the temporal priority of either. Thus the intellect from without *qua* object of thought remains an abiding and illuminating presence throughout the increase and completion of the human intellect.

112.5: There appears to be a break in the manuscript, as the participle "wishing" has no proper referent, unless we prefer with Moraux (1967 and 1984) to see here a reference to Aristotle of Mytilene, whom Moraux supposes in both these studies to be the "Aristotle" of 110.4. The section from 112.5 to 113.24 may be a fragment imperfectly interpolated into the *De Intellectu.* See Introduction pp. 23, 26-31 for a discussion of this difficulty.

112.9: * "as a substance in a substance" (ὡς οὐσία ἐν οὐσίᾳ) Moraux (1984) 418 sees a Stoicizing tendency in this passage, both because of the omnipresence of the intellect from without and because of this phrase, which appears to suggest the Stoic doctrine of total interpenetration of body by body. Gottschalk (1985) 126 replies: "Alexander's assertion that Aristotle [*sc.* of Mytilene; see Introduction pp. 22-31] allowed himself to be too much influenced by Stoicism is accepted too readily by M[oraux]. Aristotle's divine reason was incorporeal (this was the starting point of the theory) and only acted directly on the specific kind of matter capable of giving rise to a passive intellect." We may in addition observe that Alexander attacks the Stoic doctrine of total interpenetration of body by body and does not use this formula to express the doctrine, but rather σῶμα διὰ σώματος χωρεῖν, "body proceeds through body"; cf. Todd (1976) 81-88.

** "fire or something like it emerges from the mixture" (112.12). The reader is directed to Moraux (1984) 418-419 for a discussion of the ideas presented in this passage, their origins and affinities. The author adapts from the biological writings of Aristotle the notion that the soul uses as instrument the innate warmth of the organism for various life functions to the doctrine of intellect.

113.6: Various consequences that would flow from the imma- nence of the intellect from without are considered. Three Aris- totelian doctrines come into play: (1) the divine intellect is the highest cause of motion; (2) coming-to-be and passing-away in the sublunary world are caused by the motion of the heavenly bodies, especially the sun; (3) nature is in its own sphere the principle of movement.

There are two ways of interpreting the doctrine that the author means to criticize: (1) This intellect alone controls the world. Yet since coming-to-be and passing-away in this world follow the movements of the heavenly bodies, this intellect must direct itself in accordance with them. (2) The omnipresent intellect and the orderly motion of the heavenly bodies together govern the sublunary world. This contains two possible consequences: (a) The coming-to-be of earthly things is the joint effect produced by the sun and the immanent divine intellect; (b) Nature comes to be through the influence of the movements of the heavenly bodies and, together with the immanent divine intellect, governs the things of this world. It is not clear whether a discussion of these constructions and consequences is advanced by the source which our author wishes to criticize, or by the author himself. See Moraux (1984) 419-420.

113.12-24 : The author rejects the views of the source that is the object of his criticism in preference for orthodox Aristotelianism. The first of these views, 113.12-14, is a Stoic testimonium (SVF 2.1038). For a discussion, see Moraux (1984) 421-423, but see above on 112.9 on the subject of Moraux's detection of Stoicism in that source. The importance of the views advanced by this source for the subsequent history of philosophy is determined by the fact that it was not perceived that the author (thought to be Alexander) was criticizing this source; rather, its doctrine was conflated with that of the rest of the *De Intellectu* (see Gilson 9; Moraux [1984] 423-425).

113.18 : 113.18-24 on the question of whether intellect would have to change place seems not to belong here and would better suit the context at 112.5-11 as part of the exposition of the view criticized at 113.12ff. (see Introduction p. 31).

Themistius

Paraphrase of *De Anima* 3.4-8

Translated by
Robert B. Todd

THEMISTIUS: PARAPHRASE OF *DE ANIMA* 3.4-8

<PARAPHRASE OF 3.4¹>

93.32 (429a10-13): The part of the soul that we use for reasoning² and action may be spatially separate (as PLATO thought when he established reason [*94*] in the head, with emotion in the heart, and appetite in the liver), or not spatially distinct from the other faculties of the soul but separated only in thought; but what must be considered about it here is what distinguishes it from the faculties already described (and particularly from the imagination),³ and how thinking occurs at all.

94.5 (429a13-15): Now if thinking is analogous to perceiving (for the soul, as we also said earlier,⁴ makes judgments and becomes acquainted with [things] through both of these), then the intellect, too, would be in some way affected by the objects of thought, just as perception is by the objects of perception, and here too "would be affected" has to be understood in just the same way [as with perception].⁵ It is, in other words, more appropriate to say that [the intellect] would be "completed" to the fullest extent by

---

¹ In the earliest manuscripts the paraphrase of 3.4 is the conclusion of the "fifth discussion" (i.e., the paraphrase of *De Anima* 3.1-4). The division of Themistius' paraphrase into seven books (*logoi* in Greek) is confirmed in the Arabic tradition by the *Kitāb al-fihrist*; see Peters (1968a) 40.

² *theôria*; "reason" in the next clause is *ho logos*.

³ On the role of imagination (*phantasia*) in thinking cf. below 113.14-114.2 (on 3.7, 431a14-17, 431b2-10) and 115.35-116.23 (on 3.8, 432a3-14). On Themistius' account of *phantasia* see Todd (1981).

⁴ Cf. Aristotle *De Anima* 427a19-21.

⁵ Cf. *De Anima* 2.5, 418a3; cf. also 97.11-24 below where, as here, "being affected" is contrasted with the "completion" (*teleiôsis*), or actualization, that occurs in thinking. For perception distinguised from physical "affection" (*pathos*) cf. Themistius *In De Anima* 56.39-57.10, 77.34-78.10, and with particular reference to *phantasia* 92.19-23.

being advanced from potentiality to actuality.[6] And it is obvious that [it is advanced] from potentiality. That is why we do not always think,[7] nor even always think the same things rather than different things at different times; this in fact is a sign that this intellect exists in potentiality, since there can be no transition from one activity to another unless a potentiality remains to display the different activities.[8]

94.13 (429a15-18): The potential intellect must, then, be impervious to "affection" as that is spoken of primarily; also not have a shape of its own but be capable of receiving every form; be potentially such [as form] but not [identical with] it; and have the same relation to objects of thought as perception does to objects of perception. And as the latter [i.e., perception *qua* potentiality][9] is in actuality not even any of the things that it perceives, neither must this type of intellect be in actuality any of the things that are being thought. Since it thinks all things, it must, therefore, be in potentiality all things, i.e., not have a form or shape of its own.

94.20 (429a18-22): ANAXAGORAS[10] was not, then, mistakenly dreaming in making the intellect unmixed, and of a nature

---

[6] Reading *malista* at 94.9 (with MS Q, the medieval Latin version, and Spengel) for *mallon*. For the notion of "leading" (*agein*) that Themistius has restated here in a more overtly teleological form by the compound verb "advance" (*proagein*) cf. Aristotle *De Anima* 2.5, 417b10, and *Metaphysics* 9., 1051a30; see also *De Intellectu* 108.1, 110.12 and 110.32.

[7] Cf. 98.6 and 115.8-9 below for this as a deficiency of the potential intellect.

[8] The potentiality characterized here is the state of possessing thoughts (*hexis*) that precedes the activity of the active intellect. This is evident in the analogy with perception that also involves a development from a state (such as knowing something) to an activity (such as actively contemplating what is known); cf. *De Anima* 2.5, 417a22-417b2 *passim*. The present claim, therefore, depends on the account of the intellect as a state of possession (*hexis*) at 95.9-32, and on the later account of its actualization at 98.19-99.10.

[9] This gloss is justified by Aristotle's use of *to aisthêtikon* (literally "the capacity for perception") at 429a17.

[10] At Diels-Kranz 59A100 *De Anima* 429a18-20 is cited with reference to 59B12. Themistius has split this sentence and linked Anaxagoras only with the claim that the intellect is unmixed. Cf. also his version of Aristotle's earlier report about Anaxagoras at 405a13-19 at *In De Anima* 13.14-21.

different from everything that it becomes acquainted with. For in that way it would very easily become acquainted with [all things], as there would be nothing of its own "to intrude" (*paremphaino-menon* 429a20), i.e., coexist with it. The form inherent to it, that is, would exclude and obstruct the other [forms] as though they belonged to other things. An intellect of this sort must, therefore, have no nature or form of its own except its capacity to comprehend the natures and forms that belong to other things and, through being naturally disposed to grasp all things, have no determinate form.

94.27 (429a22-27): That [part] of the soul called the intellect (by "intellect" I mean that by which the soul reasons and holds beliefs, not that [intellect] that we often mistakenly apply to the imagination too[11]) is in actuality, therefore, none of the things that exist before it thinks one [of them]. So it is reasonable that it also not be mixed with the body, as mixture involves a body in relation to a body. And what exists as a body must exist in actuality and have a shape of its own. But the intellect could not, like perception, use the body even as an organ; indeed it would in that way share in the organ's quality, and as that quality would always coexist with its activities it would exclude the other forms.

94.34 (429a29-429b5): This is obvious above all from the faculty of perception. This is not a body, but since in all cases it uses bodily organs, it shares in how they are affected. And this is clear in the case of the organs of perception; for when the organs are more intensely moved by intense objects of perception (e.g., hearing by loud sound, or sight by brilliant colour, or smell by pungent odour) they can no longer [*95*] easily apprehend objects of perception that are of reduced intensity and more indistinct. Instead, the trace of the stronger impulse persists to block out the more indistinct and weaker one. When, however, the intellect thinks some "intense" object of thought, it thinks inferior things

[11] Cf. Aristotle *De Anima* 3.3, 428a1-2, with Themistius 89.27-29, and also Aristotle *De Anima* 3.10, 433a9-10.

not to a lesser, but to an even greater, extent. That, then, is why there is no perception without body, whereas the intellect is separate from body altogether.[12]

95.5 (429a27-29): And those who say that the soul is a place of forms are quite correct, even if they misuse the term "place," not allowing that it is neither the whole soul but just the two faculties by which we think and by which we perceive, nor is it place that can surround,[13] rather than in some way become, what it thinks and what it perceives.

95.9 (429b5-9):[14] Now this potential intellect comes into existence even among infants. But when it is able to hunt out[15] the universal from the objects of perception and the images derived from them, and from training involving these, and to group together what is similar among dissimilar things, and what is identical among different things, it becomes at that stage a more complete intellect, analogous to someone with knowledge[16] who has organized[17] the theorems of his body of knowledge and is able

---

[12] Cf. 104.29-105.4 below where this material is reintroduced in the excursus to emphasize the separability of the potential intellect in a more radical reconstruction.

[13] Aristotle's standard definition of place; cf., for example, *Physics* 4.4, 212a20-21.

[14] This whole passage (95.9-32) should be compared with Alexander *De Anima* 81.13-85.10, and Themistius *In Analytica Posteriora, ad* 2.19 *passim*, but especially 65.12-66.3. Unlike Alexander who identifies the formation of universals as the province of the "material intellect" (*De Anima* 85.10), Themistius follows the immediate Aristotelian text and describes a transition from a disposition for thought to the activity of thinking. Neither here nor in the paraphrase of *Analytica Posteriora* 2.19, is the role of the intellect in actuality mentioned. The exposition at 98.19-99.10 below is thus a second version of this passage.

[15] *thêreuein* (95.11). Cf. Aristotle *Analytica Posteriora* 88a3 where this verb is used in an account of demonstration to describe the pursuit of the universal. Cf. also Plato, *Phaedo* 66a3 (cf. 66c2) where it is used of discovering the forms. It importantly implies that this intellect in a "state of possession" (*hexis*) is engaged in activity.

[16] Cf. this analogy with that used by Aristotle with reference to perception at *De Anima* 2.5, 417a22-417b2.

[17] *suneilêchôs* (95.14). Ballériaux (111 note 1) suggested reading *sun-*

to be active on his own by handling each of them personally, without the need for any external instruction or training. At that stage too, therefore, the intellect is in potentiality, yet not in just the same way as before it learnt or made discoveries. For it is [now] endowed with a kind of vision[18] not previously present, one able to see similar and dissimilar things, and what is identical and different, and what is consistent and inconsistent. And at that stage it can itself think itself;[19] for the intellect is nothing but its thoughts. Thus by becoming identical with what is being thought it thinks itself too at that stage.

[*95.21*]: So when it has only the state of possessing [thoughts], its thoughts are as though set aside.[20] But when it is active, it coincides with what is thought, and as would be expected it thinks itself at that stage; for it is itself the things that it thinks. For just as knowledge is the theorems that are the objects of knowledge (geometry, that is, being nothing other than the geometrical theorems), so too is the intellect its thoughts. And as long as the state of possessing [thoughts] is itself inactive, so too are the theorems, but when the state is moved and is active, it is active in all respects towards one of its own theorems, and it becomes identical with what it is thinking about.[21] The knowledge that a

---

eilêphôs here, but the *lectio difficilior* is defensible. The verb means literally "join by lot with," and is a metaphor used by Plato (*Timaeus* 18e2; *Politicus* 266c4, e6). Since Themistius has a penchant for Platonic metaphor, he has no doubt adopted this term as an alternative for *sunagein* (95.11), although the underlying idea suggests a more random form of coordination than would be expected in this context.

[18] Cf. Themistius *In Analytica Posteriora* 65.13-15 where the potential intellect is compared to an "irrational and undiscriminating vision" that matures as a rational animal develops; also cf. Alexander *De Anima* 85.22.

[19] Here, and at 95.21, 23, and 32 Themistius has the reading *de hauton* at *De Anima* 429b9; cf. Owens *passim* for a defence of it, and see Commentary on *De Intellectu* 108.3.

[20] *apokeimena* (95.22); cf. Alexander *De Anima* 86.5-6.

[21] This passage is neutral as to what kind of thinking is involved in this actualization. At 99.1-10 below it is represented as a transition to discursive reasoning, as also at 109.4-7, where the transition is from the separate apprehension of the items in the categories to their combination in true and false propositions. At *In Analytica Posteriora* 65.28-66.3 Themistius envisages it as

triangle has two right angles is, in other words, the theorem and
reasoning by which the triangle is demonstrated as having two
right angles. In this way the intellect too, when inactive, is said
to have the state of possessing thoughts, but when active towards
one of its thoughts is at that time identical with what is being
thought, and by thinking that thing thinks itself too. (The
difference between this sort of intellect and the faculty of perceptual imagination must be explained in due course after distinguishing the nature of each of the [aspects of the intellect] that
have been described.)[22]

95.35 (429b10-11): Now water and what it is to be water are
different.[23] While water, that is, is the compound of form and
matter, what it is to be water is the form of water, and that in
respect of which water exists; for each is characterized not in
respect of its matter but in respect of its shape. [*96*] It is the same
too with artefacts. A house and what it is to be a house are
different, as are a statue and what it is to be a statue. While a
house is the shape together with the stones, planks and clay, what
it is to be a house is the shape and particular combination [of the
matter]. Similarly, while a statue too is the shape together with
the stone and bronze, what it is to be a statue is the form of the
statue.

96.5 (429b11-12): But this is not the same in all cases, for in
some they are identical, as with a point and what it is to be a
point, or anything completely immaterial and uncompounded,
where the definition of the essence and the form in respect of
which it exists are identical with the nature of the object in its
entirety.

---

a transition from mere naming, and thinking the things that are named, to
combinations and discursive reasoning, and finally to the formation of universal
judgments.
   [22] This probably looks ahead to 113.32-114.30.
   [23] Aristotle's other example, magnitude and what it is to be magnitude
(429b10), is omitted.

96.8 (429b12-16): If this is indeed the case, then (1) when we judge[24] the form taken together with the matter (e.g., cold and wet together with matter, as in our judgment of water in its entirety—water being by definition the ratio of these qualities and their combination with matter), and [in such cases] judge water in its entirety, or flesh in its entirety, the faculty of perception (even more so its yoke-fellow imagination) is adequate for us. But (2) when we examine what it is to be water and what it is to be flesh, that which makes the judgment is quite different, or is [the same thing] in a different state. For perhaps just as there has to be one faculty to judge that sweet differs from yellow,[25] so too this faculty that judges that water and what it is to be water are different must also be one, and must apprehend them both, but in two different states: (1) when it inspects matter along with the form, and (2) when it extracts the form separately. For water, that is, it needs the imagination to report [from perception], but for what it is to be water it is self-sufficient.

96.21 (429b16-18): So just as if the same line were both straight and bent you would describe it as the same, yet in two different states, so too[26] would you [describe] the intellect both when it grasps the body as compounded, and when it grasps just the form itself (i.e., the shape). [The intellect], that is, is assimilated to the things that it thinks about, and becomes sometimes as if compounded (when it thinks what is compounded), yet at other times as if uncompounded (when it extracts just the form). In the latter case it resembles the straight line, in the former the bent one. (While PLATO likens the activities of the intellect to the "smooth-

---

[24] Themistius converts Aristotle's impersonal *krinei* (429b13, 15) into this personal form here (96.9) and at 96.10 and 12, as does Hamlyn's translation, though at 96.15 and subsequently he takes the intellect to be the implied subject. Lowe 20-21 argues for the incompatibility of these alternatives, but ignores (his note 15) the fact that Themistius (of whom he cites only 96.15-27) employs both rather than the second which he (Lowe) favours.

[25] A reference back to *De Anima* 3.2, 426b17-23 (cf. Themistius 85.11-20 *ad loc.*) where Aristotle in fact speaks of distinguishing sweet from white.

[26] Omitting *de* at 96.22 with MS Q and the medieval Latin version.

running" and the "straight[-running]" [circles],[27] ARISTOTLE compares them to a line that is both bent and straight. This is because the intellect becomes as it were double instead of single when it inspects the matter along with the shape.)

96.30 (429b18-22): Also with things spoken of by abstraction some resemble water, others what it is to be water, for among these too the straight and what it is to be straight are different, and the straight is accompanied by extension, as with snubness (extension being the substrate of the straight), while what it is to be straight is the definition of the straight. In the case of these abstract objects the intellect seems to judge both, meaning by "both" that which is compounded from the substrate and the form, as well as the form itself. But even then it is not [always] in the same state, but with these too it is sometimes as if uncompounded, while at other times as though compounded. For even if one [type of] matter underlies perceptible bodies, and another the things spoken of by abstraction,[28] we would still say that with the latter too the intellect's reasoning [*97*] was less compounded at one time, but more compounded at another. So when the intellect inspects bodies it needs the faculty of perception, as it cannot judge on its own, in complete detachment from perception, what is water or flesh. But for the triangular and the straight the intellect is more self-sufficient in that just as the objects are separable from matter, so too is the reasoning of the intellect. So just as they can be separated in thought alone, but could not exist on their own, so too the intellect sets about separating them in thought alone.

97.8 (429b22-31): In one way ANAXAGORAS spoke about the intellect correctly, in another he did not: for while he offered a correct interpretation by making the intellect completely unmixed with matter,[29] he was wrong to neglect to instruct us on how it

---

[27] Cf. *Timaeus* 37b7 and c2 where these epithets occur for, respectively, the circles of the Same and the Different.

[28] That is, intelligible matter; cf. Lowe 22. It is briefly identified at 114.11 below.

[29] Cf. Diels-Kranz 59B12.

will think all things when it is like this, if indeed to think is to be affected. Nothing, that is, is affected unless it shares in matter, but this [matter] must be a substrate shared both by what is affected and by what produces an affection. And so it is not just anything that is affected by anything (e.g., a line by a sound), but [only] things that also share in the same matter.[30] But since ANAXAGORAS did not make this distinction, we must again review distinctions that we have already often drawn.[31] I mean that if "being affected" is not spoken of in its primary sense with reference to perception, is this not all the more so in the case of the intellect? Perception does at least use bodily [organs], and so would share a substrate with what produces affections (with the objects of perception, I mean); it is after all by using body that it is moved by bodies. The intellect, on the other hand, is, as has been explained, potentially all objects of thought yet is in actuality nothing until it thinks. It is, therefore, further removed from being affected [than perception] in that it does not even acquire a determinate nature.[32]

97.21 (429b31-430a2): Instead, with the intellect you get the same result as where letters are written on a tablet that has nothing actually written on it. Here you would call what is written a "completion" of the tablet, not an "affection," since it has acquired this as the [purpose] that it has come into existence for. When the intellect, that is, is active <towards>[33] the objects of thought, it is not affected but completed, so that in this respect it is unmixed and uncompounded. For in general the potential intellect, as ARISTOTLE says, is in actuality none of the things that exist, and being none [of them] in actuality, it could not be affected or mixed. Being affected and being mixed, that is, belong to what is something in actuality. And intellect in actuality comes

---

[30] Cf. Aristotle *De Anima* 1.3, 407b17-19, and *De Generatione et Corruptione* 1.7, 323b29-324a5. For the example of the line and noise as incompatible cf. Alexander *De Mixtione* (SA 2.2) 229.15, and Simplicius *In Physica* (CAG 9.1) 516.27-29.

[31] Cf. 94.5-95.5 above.

[32] Cf. 94.26 above.

[33] Heinze's addition of *peri* at 97.25 is fully justified; cf. 112.23.

into existence[34] from the potential [intellect] when thoughts also come into existence for it, and at that point it is at once both intellect and object of thought. [The potential intellect] is not, therefore, affected by the objects of thought, but itself becomes [identical with] them. (And it seems that the potential intellect comes into existence only in the human soul,[35] since only that [soul's] passions also pay heed to reason and are naturally adapted to it, while this is not at all so with the other animals.)[36]

97.34 (430a2-5, 6-9): But how is [the potential intellect] at the same time both intellect and object of thought? And is it so in the same respect, or does it become intellect in one respect and object of thought in another? Now in the case of the things without matter[37] that which thinks and that which is being thought are identical (theoretical knowledge being identical with what is known in that way), but in the case of the enmattered forms the object of thought is one thing, the intellect another. For, as we know, neither are these (the enmattered forms, I mean) [*98*] by nature objects of thought, but the intellect makes them objects of thought by severing them from matter, and they are objects of thought in potentiality, not in actuality. This is because they are in a suitable state for being thought, not because their nature can in itself be thought. It is reasonable, then, that such things are

---

[34] Themistius does not at this point say that this development depends on something already existing in actuality; that additional point is made implicitly at 98.7-8, and explicitly at 98.28-30.

[35] Cf. also 98.15, 35, and 103.5, 13 below for the same emphasis.

[36] In the excursus at 107.7-16 below, this claim is used to justify the existence of a special intellect (the passive) associated with practical reasoning involving the passions.

[37] Berti 147 with note 32, rightly argues that the phrase "without matter" (*aneu hulês*) here (430a3) and at 430b30 (cf. Themistius 112.23), refers to the "immaterial essences of material realities", and not to the special class of immaterial forms such as Themistius has in mind (cf. also 114.31-32). See also Lowe 24. At *In De Anima* 8.24-31 (commenting on 403b9-16) Themistius has a trichotomy of forms that are (i) in matter, (ii) apart from it, and (iii) "really forms" (8.30). The latter are the equivalent of the immaterial forms identified here, "separate both in definition and in mode of existence (*hupostasis*)" (8.30-31). See also the commentary on *De Intellectu* 108.14 above.

thought, though not that they think, ⟨and that while each of them is an object of thought, it is not intellect⟩.[38]

98.4 (430a5-6): This intellect (the one in potentiality, I mean) is a potential object of thought in just the same way as it is a potential intellect. That is why it does not always think, and why through thinking continuously it grows tired.[39] Potentiality, that is, underlies it, so that it is not even always an object of thought but so [only] when it assembles its thoughts.[40] But if there is some intellect entirely without potentiality, it will always be at once both intellect and object of thought.[41] It is this intellect that we indeed discuss when we begin again.

SIXTH DISCUSSION OF THEMISTIUS ON THE SOUL
⟨PARAPHRASE OF 3.5 (430a10-23)[42]⟩

98.12 (430a10-14): Since each thing that comes into existence through nature[43] has its potentiality first and its completion[44]

---

[38] The supplement after *ou* at 98.4 proposed by Browne on the basis of the Arabic translation and adopted here is: *kai noêton men hekaston, nous de ou.*

[39] "Grows tired" (*kamnei*, 98.6). Cf. Aristotle *Metaphysics* 9.8, 1050b24-27 for the same verb in a related context; there the heavenly bodies do not "grow tired" because their movement has no potentiality for opposites. Cf. also *Metaphysics* 12 (*Lambda*).9, 1074b28-29 for the principle that continuous thought is "wearisome" (*epiponon*) if thinking is a potentiality; cf. Themistius *ad loc.* 31.7-9. The activity of the intellect in actuality is, by contrast, is "unwearying" (*akamatos*); cf. 99.38 below.

[40] That is, in the intellect *qua* state of possessing thoughts, where "assembling" is the precondition for activity; cf. 99.2-10 below on the transition from this state to the activity of thinking.

[41] Cf. 100.3-4 below where this claim is made explicitly about the intellect in actuality.

[42] The sentence at 430a23-25 (cf. 101.10-12) is not discussed until the excursus.

[43] As editors note, Themistius must not have read *hôsper* ("just as") before Aristotle's phrase "in the whole of nature" (430a10). Whether it was absent from the text he used, or whether he omitted it for the grammatical reasons proposed by Ross (ed. with comm. *ad loc.*), the net effect is that he sees the relation between the two intellects as directly conforming to the general principles of natural change.

[44] "Completion" (*teleiotês*, 98.13). Cf. Todd (1974) 213-214 on the use of this term as an alternative for *eidos* or *energeia* in later Greek philosophy.

later, and is not restricted to its natural adaptability and potentiality (for then it would have them from nature in vain), it is
obvious that the human soul too does not [just] advance to having
the potential intellect, i.e., to being naturally fitted for thinking.[45]
Instead, the goal for the sake of which it was so prepared by
nature necessarily succeeds the natural adaptability. Thus the
potential intellect must be completed, yet nothing is completed
through itself but [only] through another thing. Therefore "it
is necessary that these differences exist in the soul too"
(430a13-14); that is, that while one intellect must be in potentiality, the other must exist in actuality, and as complete and not
at all in potentiality and by natural endowment, but as an intellect
existing in actuality which, by being combined[46] with the potential
intellect and advancing it to actuality, perfects the intellect that is
in a state of possessing [thoughts],[47] [i.e.], the one in which the
universal objects of thought and bodies of knowledge exist.

98.24 (430a12-13): The potential house and the potential statue
(i.e., stones and bronze) could not, that is, receive the shape of
the house or that of the statue unless a craft fastened[48] its own
power (i.e., imposed the form belonging to the craft) on to
materials fitted for this purpose, and so brought the house and
statue to perfection as compounds. Similarly, the potential intellect must be completed by some other intellect that is already
complete, i.e., in actuality, not in potentiality.[49] By moving the

----

[45] The two levels identified here correspond to the potential intellect in its
primary form as an endowment of infants (95.9-10), and as the intellect *qua*
"state" of possessing thought (*hexis*) into which it develops.

[46] *sumplakeis* (98.22). The term may be metaphorical (meaning "inter-
locked," "woven together"; cf. Plato *Timaeus* 36e2), but it is evident from
116.12 below (following 432a11) that it was interchangeable with the standard
verb for combining, *suntithêmi*.

[47] *ton kath'hexin noun* (98.23).

[48] *endousa* (98.27). Cf. Plato, *Timaeus* 69e4 (= 106.27 below) where this
verb is used to describe the insertion of the mortal soul in the breast; cf. also
Timaeus 73b3-4.

[49] An application of the wider principle of the temporal priority of actuality
that closely echoes Aristotle *Metaphysics* 9.8, 1049b24-25.

potential intellect analogously to the craft [this intellect] brings to completion the soul's natural adaptability for thinking, and fully equips its state of possessing [thoughts].[50] "And this intellect is separate, unaffected and unmixed" (430a17-18). As for the intellect that we call potential, even if we fully apply the same terms to it, it is still far more innate[51] to the soul (not every soul, I mean, but only the human soul).

98.35 (430a15-17): And as light when added to potential vision and potential colours produces both actual vision [*99*] and actual colours, so too this actual intellect advances the potential intellect, and not only makes it actual intellect but also equips its potential objects of thought as actual objects of thought. These are the enmattered forms, i.e., the universal thoughts assembled from particular objects of perception. Up to this point the potential intellect is unable to distinguish between them, or make transitions between distinct thoughts,[52] or combine and divide them.[53] Instead, like a treasury[54] of thoughts, or indeed like matter, it deposits the imprints from perception and imagination by means of memory.[55] But when the productive intellect[56] encounters it and takes over this "matter" of thoughts, the potential intellect

---

[50] It does not equip it *with* such a state; that, as 95.9-20 shows, is independently established. Cf. 99.2-3 where the same verb (*kataskeuazein*) is used with reference to the process of converting preexistent potential objects of thought to actual objects of thought.

[51] *sumphuês* (98.34). Its being "more innate" than the intellect in actuality must be understood in light of its status as the "forerunner" of that intellect in the soul; cf. below 105.33-34 and 106.13.

[52] Cf. 94.12-13 above where the potential intellect is represented as the necessary condition for making such transitions.

[53] Cf. 109.4-18 (on 3.6, 430a26-31) below for Themistius' account of these operations.

[54] Cf. Themistius *In De Anima* 56.20-21 (on 2.5, 417b22-24) for a description of the accumulation of universals as "storing treasure" (*thêsaurize-sthai*). The source of the metaphor may be Plato *Phaedrus* 276d3.

[55] Memory was omitted from the earlier account of the formation of universals at 95.10-12; it is a standard component of such genetic accounts; cf. Alexander *De Anima* 83.5-6 and Themistius *In Analytica Posteriora* 63.14-17.

[56] *poiêtikos nous* (99.8). This is the first occurence of the expression in Themistius' discussion. See Introduction p. 32 and note 106.

becomes one with it, and becomes able to make transitions, and to combine and divide thoughts, and to observe thoughts from [the perspective of] one another.

99.11 (430a12-13, 14-15): The relation that a craft has to its matter is, then, just that which the productive intellect too has to the potential intellect, and in this way the latter becomes all things, while the former produces all things.[57] That is why it is also in our power to think whenever we wish.[58] For <the productive intellect> is not outside <the potential intellect as> the craft <is external>[59] to the matter (as bronze-working is to bronze and carpentry to wood), but the productive intellect sinks into the whole of the potential intellect, as though the carpenter and the bronze-worker did not control their wood and bronze externally but could pervade it totally.[60] For this is how the actual intellect too is added to the potential intellect and becomes one with it. In other words, that [which is compounded] from matter and form is one,[61] and moreover has the two definitions, both that of matter and that of creativity, by in one way becoming all things, but in another producing all things. For it somehow becomes the actual objects [that it thinks] by being active in its thinking, and the one [aspect] of it, where the plurality of its thoughts is, resembles matter, whereas the other is like a craftsman.[62] For it

----

[57] Cf. 430a14-15.

[58] Cf. *De Anima* 2.5, 417b24 (with Themistius 56.23-24 *ad loc.*). Aristotle's associated claim that universals are "somehow in the soul" (417b23-24) envisages an intimate relationship analogous to that proposed here between the productive and potential intellects.

[59] The translation incorporates after *exôthen* at 99.13 the supplement proposed by Browne from the Arabic version: *tou dunamei nou ho poiêtikos, hôsper exôthen.*

[60] Cf. Aristotle *Physics* 2.8, 199b28-30 for the general notion of nature as an internal craft. This language of "total pervasion" can be described as Stoic, given that earlier in this paraphrase (35.32-33) Themistius refers to Zeno's belief that God pervaded the whole of matter.

[61] For further applications of this hylomorphic relation cf. below 100.31-37, and especially 108.32-34.

[62] The representation of Intellect as craftsman (*dêmiourgos*) is common in Plotinus; cf. 5.1 [10].8.5-6 with Atkinson *ad loc.*

is in its power, when it wishes, to comprehend and give shape to its thoughts, since it is itself productive of thoughts and their originator. Hence it also particularly resembles God,[63] for God is indeed in one way the actual things that exist, but in another their provider.[64] And the intellect is far more estimable insofar as it is creative than insofar as it is acted on,[65] as in all cases the productive principle is more estimable than the matter.[66]

99.26 (430a19-21): And, as I have frequently said,[67] the intellect is the same as the object of thought (just as actual knowledge is [the same as] its very object of knowledge), yet not in the same respect; rather, it is an object of thought insofar as it encompasses the potential intellect, while it is intellect insofar as it is itself in actuality. In a human being, then, the potential intellect is prior to the actual intellect,[68] given that all natural adaptability is prior in time to its actuality.[69] But in absolute terms it is not prior; for the incomplete is never prior to the complete, nor potentiality to actuality.[70]

99.32: The essence of the productive intellect is identical with its activity (430a18),[71] i.e., it does not advance from potentiality, but

[63] But it is not identical with God; cf. 102.36-103.19 in the excursus below.

[64] *chorêgos* (99.25). Cf. Plotinus 6.2 [43].20.13, and also 103.23 below, where the word is used of the productive intellect *qua* source of light.

[65] *katho paschei* (99.26). Themistius is reflecting Aristotle's *tou paschontos* (430a19). In the excursus, however, he will argue that the potential intellect is distinct from the passive (*pathêtikos*; cf. 430a24); cf. 101.5-9, and 105.13-34 below.

[66] Cf. *De Anima* 3.5, 430a18-19.

[67] Cf. 95.19-23, 31-32; 97.34-37; and 98.8-9.

[68] The inference that follows seems to represent an extrapolation from Aristotle's observations on potential knowledge at 430a20-21 to the relationship between the potential and actual intellects. Cf., however, note 96 below.

[69] Cf. 98.12-19 above.

[70] Cf. Aristotle *Metaphysics* 9.8, 1049b17-24, and 106.9-14 below.

[71] Ballériaux remarks that in making this statement "Thémistius est plus près des *Ennéades* que du *De Anima*," and refers to Plotinus 5.3 [49].5.41-42 and its context (142). But in elaborating this Aristotelian insight in this and the next paragraph in Plotinian language Themistius does not abandon his basic Aristotelian frame of reference.

its nature is of the same kind as its activity, and this[72] intellect, as already stated earlier too, is really "separate, unaffected, and unmixed" (430a17-18), "not thinking at one time but not at another" (430a22). For though this [activity] persists when it adopts[73] the potential intellect, this is exclusively what it is (430a22-23) when it itself exists in respect of itself.

[*99.37*]:[74] And it is an activity that is unceasing, untiring, immortal and eternal. As both intellect and object of thought [*100*] it is precisely the same, not at all in respect of successively distinct things.[75] Nor does it exist on account of something else like the other objects of thought that the intellect in its state of possessing [thoughts] produces as objects of thought by separating them from matter. Instead, it is an object of thought on account of itself, and by the nature derived from itself it has the [properties of] being thought and of thinking.

100.4: In the potential intellect, then, where the crafts and bodies of knowledge exist, thoughts are divided [from one another]. In the actual intellect, on the other hand, (in its activity rather, given that in its case its essence is identical with its activity), they would exist in a different way, harder to describe and more divine,[76] in

---

[72] Here (99.34) the Arabic version has the equivalent of *houtos* ("this") for *houtôs* ("thus"); Browne rightly advocates adopting it in view of the parallel at 98.32-33, the passage recalled here.

[73] "Persists" (*hupomenein*) and "adopts" (*hupoballesthai*; cf. *hupoballein* IV in LSJ), carry the implication that the productive intellect is in some sense a substrate for the potential intellect. That cannot be intended, and it might have been better if the language of emanation, so prevalent in this passage, had been used here too. *Hupomenein* is, in fact, used elsewhere (94.12, 100.12) to characterize the adaptability of the *potential* intellect in discursive reasoning.

[74] Cf. Plotinus 5.9 [5].5.1-10 for a similar expansion of the basic Aristotelian claim that intellect is in essence actuality, or activity.

[75] Cf. 100.1 (*ouketi kat'allo kai allo*) with Plotinus 4.4 [28].2.23-24 where the phrase *to allo kai allo* is used to draw a contrast with the way that the soul thinks in the intelligible realm.

[76] Cf. the language used to describe this non-discursive thinking at Plotinus at 4.4 [28].1.15-16 and 19-20. For the general contrast between the "all togetherness" (*panta homou*) of forms in the intellect and their separation in the soul; cf. also Plotinus 4.4 [28].2 *passim*, and 1.1 [53].8.8, and for references

that [this intellect] does not change from one particular thing to another, nor combine or divide [thoughts], nor go through a process[77] to [reach] its acts of thinking, but it has all the forms[78] all together and entertains[79] all of them at the same time. Only in this way would its essence and its activity be, as ARISTOTLE says (430a18), identical. Were it to make transitions like those engaged with bodies of knowledge,[80] then its essence would have to persist while its activity was altered, and that is for its essence and its activity to differ, something ARISTOTLE explicitly rejects. Indeed in this vein he says in Book One too: "discursive reasoning, loving, and hating, are not its affections" (408b25-26).[81]

<EXCURSUS TO THE PARAPHRASE OF 3.5>
<*That we are the productive intellect*>

100.16: We, then, are either the potential intellect or the actual intellect. So if in the case of everything that is compounded from

---

to the former state cf. 5.9 [5].10.10 and 3.7 [45].3 *passim*. Themistius offers only a sketchy reflection of the rich Plotinian discussions on which there has been some recent debate; see Sorabji 152-156 and Lloyd (1986). The language here also appears in Themistius' account of divine intellection in his paraphrase of Aristotle's *Metaphysics* 12 (*Lambda*); see the references at note 218 below.

[77] *oude diexodôi proschrômenou* (100.8). The term *diexodos* can mean a narrative in classical Greek, and it is that sense of a cumulative and discursive process that Themistius is trying to convey. Plotinus uses the term frequently in this sense, and with reference to the intellect; cf. 4.4 [28].1.15 and 6.7 [38].13.48.

[78] "All" must include both immaterial and enmattered forms, to use the dichotomy introduced at 97.35-37 above; cf. also note 218, and 103.30-32 below where the productive intellect is said to think independently everything that potential intellect comes to think.

[79] The verb used here, *proballesthai*, is elsewhere employed by Themistius to describe the mind's presentation of images to itself (*In De Anima* 93.3 and 114.2; cf. Aristotle *De Insomniis* 458b22). To the extent that it suggests such a process it is misleading; on the other hand, it effectively indicates the self-contemplation involved where, as with the entertainment of images, there is no immediate dependency on external situations.

[80] *hoi epistêmones* (100.11). This intellect, like the Aristotelian God (cf. 102.33-35 below), cannot be identified with the inferential type of reasoning involved in special bodies of knowledge.

[81] These affections belong to a passive intellect that can be distinguished from the potential intellect. Cf. 101.5-37 and 105.13-34 below.

the potential and the actual the this[82]and what it is <to be> this
are distinct, then the I[83] and what it is to be me would also be
distinct, and while I am the intellect compounded from the
potential and the actual [intellects], what it is to be me is derived
from the actual [intellect].[84] Thus while the intellect compounded
from the potential and the actual [intellects] is writing what I am
[now] thinking through and composing, it is writing not *qua*
potential but *qua* actual [intellect], for activity from the latter is
chanelled[85] to it.

100.22 : There is nothing remarkable about the potential intellect
being unable to receive in an undivided form what the actual
intellect provides in this way, as neither in the case of [physical]
bodies does their matter receive qualities in an undivided form,
although qualities are by their own definition undivided; matter
instead receives in a divided form whiteness [for example] that
is [itself] undivided.[86]

100.26 : So just as the animal and what it is to be an animal are
distinct, and what it is to be an animal is derived from the soul
of the animal, so also the I and what it is to be me are distinct.
What it is to be me is, then, derived from the soul, yet from this
not in its totality—not, that is, from the faculty of perception (that
being matter for the imagination), nor again from the faculty of

---

[82] *to tode* (100.17). This could be translated less literally as "a particular
thing." The virtue of the literal translation is that it brings out the parallel with
the innovative expression "the I" (cf. next note).

[83] *to egô* (100.18). This would seem to be the first use of this locution as
a referring term. At svf 2.895, p. 245 lines 19-20 it is used only to identify *to
egô* as an expression.

[84] Moraux (1978a) 323 note 136 gathers references that set this passage in
the wider Greek philosophical tradition of identifying the soul or the intellect
as a real self. See also Himmereich 92-100 on Plotinus' use of *hemeis* and *to
hemeis* ("we," "the we") in this sense.

[85] *epocheteuetai* (100.22). The metaphor is probably derived from Plato
Phaedrus 251e3.

[86] This paragraph looks ahead to the fuller discussion of the unity of the
intellect at 103.20-104.23 below; cf. note 121. It can also be compared in broad
terms with Plotinus 5.9 [5].9, and also with 6.4 [22].7-8.

imagination (that being matter for the potential intellect), nor from the potential intellect (that being matter for the productive intellect).[87] What it is to be me is, accordingly, derived from the productive intellect alone, since this alone is form in a precise sense, and indeed this is "a form of forms"[88], and the other things are at once both substrates and forms, and nature indeed progresses by using them as forms for less estimable things, and as matter for more estimable ones. But ultimate and supreme among forms is this productive intellect, and when nature had advanced as far as it, she stopped,[89] as she had nothing else more estimable for which she could have made it a substrate.

<*The productive and passive intellects*>

100.37: We, then, [*101*] are the productive intellect, and it is reasonable for ARISTOTLE to pose for himself the problem of why we do not, therefore, remember after death whatever we think here. And the solution, entailed both by his present and by his earlier statements about the intellect, is that the productive intellect is unaffected, while the passive intellect is perishable (430a24-25).

101.5: We shall consider what he calls the passive and perishable intellect as we proceed, and the fact that he does not admit this as the potential intellect,[90] but some other intellect (which he called "common" in Book One), along with which [the productive intellect] thinks the things here [in life], and with which it

---

[87] This hierarchy in terms of form and matter has, as Mahoney (1973) 428 note 27, and (1982a) 169 note 1 observes, some analogues in Plotinus: cf. 2.4 [12].3; 3.4 [15].1; 3.9 [13].5.

[88] Cf. *De Anima* 3.8, 432a2 and note 225 below.

[89] Themistius uses exactly this language at 49.4 in his paraphrase of the account of the hierarchy of faculties in *De Anima* 2.3 to describe the superiority of the rational faculty. There, however, the language of form and matter is not employed; its application to the hierarchy of the faculties is innovative and perhaps (cf. note 87) reflects other influences.

[90] As is argued at 105.13-34 below.

reasons discursively about the things here, and to which loving, hating and remembering belong. But for now we can more strongly affirm that he believes that we are the productive intellect when he both poses a problem, and offers a solution, with the words: "But we do not remember because this [the productive intellect] is unaffected, while the passive intellect is perishable" (430a23-25). The following problem, that is, is a consequence that he also shares with all who regard the intellect as immortal: why after death do we never remember the things in life, and exchange neither friendship nor hostility, nor appear to the kin from whom we are particularly removed?[91] Hence he considers it worth solving correctly both in Book One and here, and provides the same explanation of our [productive] intellect having no memory both in what he said about it at the outset and in what he now pursues more explicitly.

101.18: He even employs almost exactly the same statements[92] when he says (1) in the former context:

> "But discursive reasoning, and loving or hating, are not an affection[93] of that thing [the productive intellect],[94] but of this thing that has it, insofar as it has it. Thus, when this too is destroyed, it [the productive intellect] neither remembers nor loves. For these did not belong to it, but to the common [intellect][95] that has perished,

---

[91] Plotinus, 4.3 [27].32-4.4 [28].1, has a more elaborate and subtle investigation of posthumous memory, and unlike Themistius can admit the retention of memory by an aspect of the surviving soul. See Pépin 176-177 for a full discussion. There is some similarity between the language at 101.13-15 and Plotinus 4.3 [27].32.1-2.

[92] Following the transposition at 101.18 *tois autois rhêmasi*, adopted by De Falco without explanation. It seems justified by the reference to *tas autas aitias* at 101.16, and the use of *tauton* at 101.28-29.

[93] Here (101.20) Themistius has *pathêma* for Aristotle's *pathê* (408b26). He employs *pathê* when this passage is repeated at 105.18 below.

[94] This supplement represents Themistius' understanding of *to noein* and *to theôrein* at 408b24.

[95] This supplement highlights Themistius' perverse interpretation of this text; i.e., instead of accepting the natural meaning of *to koinon* as the compound of the reasoning faculty and the body (the reference of "this thing" in the first sentence of the quotation), he sees it as an intellect exclusively linked with the

whereas the [productive] intellect is surely something more divine
and is unaffected" (1.4, 408b25-29).

And (2) in the present context:

"and in general neither [does the productive intellect think][96] in
time, but it is not the case that it thinks at one time but not at
another. And when it has been separated it is just what it is, and
this alone is immortal and eternal. But we do not remember
because this is unaffected, whereas the passive intellect is perishable. And without this [the passive intellect], it [the productive
intellect] thinks nothing"[97] (3.5, 430a21-25).

---

perishable body. Cf. also below 105.26-29, and note 142. De Falco's "orga-
nismo commune" follows the orthodox reading of the Aristotelian text but
obscures Themistius' exegetical intentions. For Alexander of Aphrodisias (*De
Anima* 82.10-15) the common intellect was a general form of intelligence to be
contratsted with more elaborate forms of ratiocination.

[96] This supplement extracts Themistius' interpretation of the clause "and in
general not even in time" (*holôs de oude chronôi*) at 430a21. This is normally
taken with the preceding sentence (20-21) and regarded as a further definition
of the way in which potential knowledge is not prior (e.g. "but not prior even
in time in general," in Hamlyn's rendering). Such a claim would of course have
no bearing on the present context where the productive and passive intellects
are being contrasted. Indeed at 101.28 below, our (*1a*), Themistius represents
the productive intellect as not thinking in time, in contrast with the description
of the common intellect's discursive thinking in (*1b*). Later, however, Themistius speaks of the potential intellect being prior in time in the individual (like
potential knowledge at 430a20-21), and then adds (as he does not in a similar
passage at 99.30-33; cf. note 68) "but indeed not even in time" (106.11-12).
This looks like a use of the clause at 430a21, as it is normally understood.

[97] This would seem to be Themistius' reading of this notoriously difficult
sentence at 430a25. In support note that (1) at 101.7 he says that the productive
intellect thinks "the things [sc. in life; cf. 101.14-15]" in company with the
passive intellect; (2) at 102.2-4 he paraphrases *De Anima* 1.4, 408b28-29 as
saying that the productive intellect cannot reason discursively or remember when
the common intellect is destroyed; (3) at 102.24 he expands the present
sentence into the claim that "without it, it thinks nothing *nor does it remember*",
where it is obviously the productive intellect that does not remember. All this
indicates that Themistius takes 430a25 as claiming that the productive intellect
thinks in the same way as the passive intellect only when it is linked with it. This
would be the corollary of the main thesis of this section, that it does not think
in this way (or remember) when dissociated from it after death. This reading
does, however, require that Themistius take "thinks" *noei* (430a25) to refer to
the passive intellect's "discursive" thinking, otherwise identified by *dianoeisthai*,
as at *De Anima* 1.4, 408b25-26; cf. e.g. 100.14, 20; 101.8, 102.3.

101.27: [The following pairs of statements], that is, are <almost>[98] exactly the same:

> (*1a*) (430a21-22) "neither does [the productive intellect] think in time" and "it is not the case that it thinks at one time but not at another"; AND (*1b*) it does not reason discursively but discursive reasoning belongs to a distinct thing to which also belongs not thinking always but [thinking] in time.[99]
>
> (*2a*) (430a22-23) "and when it has been separated it is just what it is, and this alone is immortal and eternal"; AND (*2b*) (408b29) "whereas the [productive] intellect is surely something more divine and is unaffected."
>
> (*3a*) (430a23-25) "But we do not remember because this is unaffected, whereas the passive intellect is perishable. And without this [the passive intellect], it [the productive intellect] thinks nothing." AND (*3b*) (408b27-29) "Thus when this too is destroyed, it [the productive intellect] neither remembers nor loves. For these did not belong to it, but to the common [intellect] that has perished."

101.36: It follows that all who believed that they could impugn the philosopher were misled, i.e., those[100] who thought that he both stated and solved the problem incorrectly.[101] [*102*]

---

[98] *schedon* is supplied before *antikrus* at 101.29 on the basis of 101.18.

[99] (*1b*) is not an Aristotelian text but an inference from *De Anima* 1.4, 408b25-29. It is an extreme example of the more adventurous exegetical technique followed in the excursus.

[100] Who are "these"? It may be irrelevant to ask, since in ancient polemics an alternative thesis is often vaguely attributed to a group. On the other hand, Themistius does mention (at 102.17-18) the question of why the perishable intellect does not remember the activities of the imperishable intellect prior to its birth, and calls this query "a fool's errand." Now this might have been the question that these opponents (as well as some Aristotelian commentators; cf. note 106) thought that Aristotle should have asked and answered. Their solution may have been that oblivion results from the soul's association with the body (a Platonic and Neoplatonic position; cf. Plotinus 5.1 [10].1.1-3 with Atkinson *ad loc.*). A Platonist could then have invoked the theory of recollection to explain how we can in fact recall what we knew before birth. Perhaps Themistius is trying to exclude this possibility at 102.17-18.

[101] The text at 101.37 needs a negative idea of some kind. The translation follows Moraux (1978a) 324 note 137 in reading *kakôs* for the first *kai*.

<*Supplementary discussion*>

102.1: Why, then, do we never remember the objects of the productive intellect's activity on its own, i.e., before it contributed to our constitution?[102] For he does say that on the destruction of the common intellect the productive intellect can neither reason discursively nor remember (408b25-29): "For discursive reasoning[103] did not belong to it but to the commmon [intellect] that has perished" (408b28-29). Thus when he repeats "but we do not remember because this is unaffected, whereas the passive intellect is perishable" (430a23-25), he makes us the productive intellect, while saying that the common intellect perishes, and that that is why, being immortal, we cannot remember the activities that we shared with the mortal intellect.[104] We must, then, compare both passages, and we shall find them certainly consistent with one another, and giving precise instruction on the philosopher's belief, since the following [passage] too is precisely consistent with those cited: "nothing is yet clear regarding the theoretical intellect, but this seems to be a different kind of soul, just as the eternal is [different] from the perishable" (2.2, 413b24-27).[105]

---

[102] This "constitution" (*sustasis*) is that of the productive and passive intellects; the status of the potential intellect awaits definition at 104.23-106.14 below.

[103] Here "discursive reasoning" (*dianoeisthai*) is substituted at 408b28.

[104] But if the "we" that survives is identical with the productive intellect, and has no bodily or psychological continuity with its previous state, it is questionable whether the personal pronoun can be used to refer to anything. As Rist (1966b) 15 puts it, "We do not remember after death because 'we' do not survive," and this is the natural reading of the passage. Themistius ought perhaps to have explored more deeply the nature of this surviving self, and its impersonal and collective character. His talk of an inability to remember obscures the point that it is conceptually impossible for the surviving intellect to have access to individual memories. His view that the potential intellect is permanently associated with the productive intellect by being separate from the body (105.34-106.14; 108.32-34) presumably justifies his characterizing the productive intellect as a self, rather than as a totally impersonal actuality.

[105] The idea that the productive intellect is a soul at all is an important element in the Themistian noetic. Cf. Introduction pp. 38-39, and notes 115 and 156 below.

102.13: It follows, that is, that here [in 3.5] he solves more precisely the problem that he posed and solved in a limited way in Book One [ch. 4]. In Book One his problem was not why this perishable and passive intellect does not remember the activities that the unaffected and eternal intellect undertook.[106] That was not even worth raising, as it is a complete fool's errand to work through the problem of how the intellect that perishes does not remember the activities of the imperishable intellect. The problem that is worth raising is why the intellect that is not affected and does not perish does not remember the activities that it shared with the intellect that does perish. He solves it (1) by saying earlier, "Thus when this too is destroyed, it [the productive intellect] neither remembers nor loves. For these did not belong to it, but to the common [intellect] that has perished" (408b27-29), and (2) by saying here, "but we do not remember because this [the productive intellect] is unaffected, whereas the passive intellect is perishable. And without this [the passive intellect], it [the productive intellect] thinks nothing" (430a23-25), nor does it remember anything.

102.24: THEOPHRASTUS poses the problem in just the same way in his examination of ARISTOTLE's views regarding the productive intellect.[107] He says:

---

[106] Several commentators have seen this as the problem being answered at *De Anima* 3.5, 430a23-25. Cf. Hicks's edition of the *De Anima* 508 for a measured discussion tending to the view that Aristotle is indeed referring to the impossibility of remembering life before birth. For the same general position as Themistius see De Corte 83, with note 2, where references to other commentators are gathered.

[107] This passage is repeated with some variants at 108.25-28 below, but 102.26 ("For ... innate") is omitted. Both passages contribute to Fragment XII in Barbotin's collection (270-271). The significance of this fragment does not fully emerge until Themistius infers (at 108.28-34) that the mixture that leads to loss of memory occurs between a *compound* of the actual and potential intellects on the one hand, and the passive (or common) intellect on the other. Since the potential and passive intellects are not distinguished (as promised at 101.5-9) until 105.13-34, this quotation is premature. Cf. also note 173 below.

"For if the faculty [of the intellect] is 'like a positive state' (430a15), then if it is innate [to the soul], it would also have [to be so] originally and perpetually. But if a later [development], with what, and how, does it come into existence? It seems, then, that if indeed it is imperishable, it is as though it does not come into existence. If in that case it is inherent [to the soul], why is it not so always? Why is there loss of memory and confusion? Is it because of the mixture [with the passive intellect]?" [108]

<Is the productive intellect the first god?[109]>

102.30: On the basis of the same passages it is justifiable to be amazed at all who believed that according to ARISTOTLE this productive intellect is either the First God, or is the premises[110] and bodies of knowledge derived from them that are subsequently present in us.

102.33: Those who believe it to be the premises, that is, have gone completely deaf, and do not even hear the philosopher crying aloud that this intellect is divine,[111] "unaffected" (430a24), and has its activity identical with its essence (430a18),[112] and that this alone is immortal, eternal and separate (430a22-23).

[108] Barbotin is correct to make this, as well as 108.28, a question, rather than the statement it is in Heinze's edition. Without this the particle *ê* would have to change abruptly from an interrogative to a declarative (cf. note 120) sense. Also the question fits with the general description of Theophrastus as "posing problems" (*aporei*, 102.26). For Themistius this question is, however, rhetorical, as his interpretation of Theophrastus at 108.30-31 below clearly shows.

[109] This section might perhaps follow more logically after 100.15 where the independent intellection of the active intellect has just (100.5-10) been characterized in terms that certainly raise the question of its identity with the Aristotelian God (cf. note 218 below). There is, however, a cross-reference to 102.11-13 at 103.6-7; also 103.20-21 provides a link with the immediately preceding section. Also at 104.23-24 there is a reference back to the problem raised at 103.24-26.

[110] At the same time the existence of such first principles can be used to demonstrate the unity of the productive intellect; cf. 103.38-104.2 below.

[111] This epithet is probably elicited from *De Anima* 1.4, 408b29 (cf. also 100.7); when used of *nous* later (114.34, 36) it is with reference to the "first" God.

[112] Cf. 100.10-14 where discursive reasoning is denied the actual intellect

102.36: As for those who believe that the productive intellect is
said by him to be the First God,[113] why on earth do they overlook
the following in this very passage?[114] [*103*] For after first saying
that in the whole of nature there is one thing that is matter, and
another that moves matter and completes it (430a10-12), he
claims that "it is necessary that these differences exist also in the
soul" (430a13-14), and that while one intellect is like this "by
becoming all things", another is so "by producing all things"
(430a14-15). For he states that an intellect like this is "in the
soul," and is like a part of the human soul that is the most
estimable.[115] This is clear too from that passage that we referred
to just above [at 102.11-13]: "nothing is yet clear regarding the
theoretical intellect, but this seems to be a different kind of soul,
just as the eternal is [different] from the perishable" (2.2,
413b24-27).

103.9: Also where he says "this alone is immortal and eternal"
(430a23) he could not be speaking with reference to the First
God, as he regards not only this [God] as immortal and eternal,
but also virtually all the capacities of the divine bodies for causing
motion that he also chooses to enumerate in his systematic

---

on just these grounds. Themistius also denies that God draws inferences "ex
praemissis manifestis" (*In Metaphysica Lambda* 33.2). In a different context
Plotinus (5.5 [32].1.38) also denies the identity of the intellect and unde-
monstrated premises.

[113] He is referring to Alexander of Aphrodisias; cf. *De Anima* 88.17-91.6.
The use of the plural is a matter of convention in polemic (cf. note 100).

[114] Cf. notes 190, 195, and 218 below on later passages that have impli-
cations for the general distinction between the actual intellect and God. The
present argument focusses very closely on the text of *De Anima* 3.5.

[115] The hesitant way in which the intellect is linked with the soul here is in
keeping with Aristotle's use of "it seems" (*eoike*) at 413b25 in the quotation that
follows in the next sentence. Cf. 103.16-17 and 107.5 for equally indefinite
characterizations of this relation. At *In De Anima* 49.8-10 (on 2.3, 415a11-12)
Themistius in fact wonders whether the *theorêtikos nous* may be "neither a
faculty nor a part of the soul but a distinct substance coming to exist as a
superior in what is inferior." All the same, the general thrust of Themistius'
position is clearly that the productive intellect is soul-like in virtue of its
hylomorphic relation to the potential intellect; cf. Introduction pp. 37-39.

treatise the *Metaphysics*.[116] In the case of the human soul and its associated faculties, however, he would be correct to define it alone as immortal in saying "and this alone is immortal" (430a23). Indeed on the basis of this same statement it can also be affirmed that the productive intellect is either some [aspect] of us, or is us.[117] It would be consistent of him, that is, to say that "this alone [is] immortal" as belonging to us, whereas to say without qualification that "this alone is immortal" would be inconsistent of him when he believes that many other things are immortal.

<*Is the productive intellect one or many?*[118]>

103.20: It is not difficult to solve these [problems] in this way; what, however, merits a really extensive examination is whether this productive intellect is one or many.

103.21: On the basis of the light with which it is compared (430a15) it would, that is, be one. For light too, of course, is one, and so too indeed is that which provides the light by which all vision among animals is advanced from potentiality to actuality. So [by this comparison] just as the imperishability of the common light has no relation to each case of vision, so the eternity of the productive intellect has no relation to each [one] of us.

103.26: If, on the other hand, there are many productive intellects, i.e., one for each of the potential intellects, on what basis will they differ from one another? For where things are the same in species, division is by matter, and the productive intellects must be the same in species, given that they all have their essence identical with their activity, and all think the same things. For if

---

[116] That is, at *Metaphysics* 12 (*Lambda*).8 *passim.*

[117] This is an inclusive disjunction. Earlier Themistius speaks of the productive intellect as "ours" (*hemôn*, 101.16), as well as being "us" (101.9-10, 102.6-7).

[118] This section offers the first statement of this issue in the exegetical tradition. The main modern discussions are by Ballériaux 150-170; Verbeke (1957) xxxix-lxii; S.B. Martin 13-17; and Bazán (1976-77) 70-73.

they do not think the same, but different, things, what is to rule out [division]? But from where will the potential intellect too think all things, if the intellect that advances it to actuality does not think all things first?[119]

103.32: Yet[120] the intellect that illuminates primarily is one, while those that are illuminated and that illuminate are, like light, more than one.[121] For while the sun is one,[122] you could speak of light as in some way divided into cases of vision. That is why ARISTOTLE makes his comparison not with the sun but with light,[123] whereas PLATO's is with the sun; i.e., he makes it analogous to the Good.[124]

---

[119] That the potential intellect does think all things is claimed at *De Anima* 3.4, 429a18 (cf. Themistius 94.18-20), and that the actual intellect "has all the forms" was claimed at 100.9 (cf. note 78). This picture of the latter as a guarantor of human thinking can be compared with some recent interpretations of Aristotle (Hartmann 268; Kahn 411-413), though interestingly both these modern scholars, in contrast with Themistius, show some sympathy for Alexander's identification of this intellect with the God of *Metaphysics* 12 (*Lambda*); see Hartmann 267 note 28, and Kahn 414.

[120] The particle *ê* ("yet") introduces the solution to the dilemma presented in the preceding two paragraphs (thus Ballériaux 151), just as it often indicates the answer to a preceding question; cf. for example, 104.25 and 116.18 below. Given this, the proposal by Merlan (1963) 50 note 3 to delete 103.32-36 as an interpolation does not seem reasonable.

[121] Since 103.26-32 rejects a plurality of *independent* productive intellects, this sentence would seem to posit a plurality of *subordinate* productive intellects. See, for example, Verbeke (1957) xliii. This subordination is to a shared productive intellect that transcends individuality; cf. 104.10-11, 20-21, and the whole discussion earlier at 100.16-26. The conjoined clause "and illuminate" is a problem, as it is not clear what can be illuminated by individual intellects in the course of their thinking; can they continue the illumination that they receive (cf. 109.5)? The clause may be a gloss.

[122] In this identification of the productive intellect as a source of light Themistius is closer to Plotinus' than to Alexander's earlier use of the imagery of light to describe intellection; cf. Schroeder (1984) on this background. The language of illumination is of course widespread in Plotinus; cf. Mahoney (1982a) 169 note 1. For Themistius cf. also *In De Anima* 25.36-27.7, a discussion of an argument from Porphyry, on which see Moraux (1978a) 307.

[123] Cf. 430a15 with 98.35-99.1 above.

[124] Cf. *Republic* 508bc. Cf. Sprague for speculation on Aristotle's reasons for not referring to a source of light in *De Anima* 3.5. It is not, of course, true, as Themistius implies, that the form of the Good in the Platonic analogy with the sun is somehow exclusively transcendent; cf. *Republic* 509b and Sprague 251.

103.36: And there is no need to be amazed if we who are compounded from the potential and the actual [intellects] are referred back to one productive intellect, and that what it is to be each of us is [derived] from that one thing.[125] Where, otherwise, are the common notions from?[126] [*104*] Where is the untaught and identical understanding of the primary definitions and primary axioms from? Mutual understanding, that is, would perhaps not even exist unless there were one intellect in which we all shared.[127] And PLATO's statement is true, that "if there was not some <feeling> that was the same, while different for different human beings, but instead one of us felt something distinct from the others, it would not be easy for him to indicate his own feeling to another" (*Gorgias* 481c5-d1).

104.6: So too with bodies of knowledge, the teacher thinks the same things as the learner; teaching and learning, that is, would not even exist unless teacher and learner had the same thought. And if, as is necessary, it is the same, then clearly the teacher also has the same intellect as that of the learner, given that in the case of the intellect its essence is identical with its activity. And surely the reason why only in the case of human beings is there teaching, learning, and mutual understanding generally, but not at all in the case of the other animals, is that the constitution of other souls is not even such that it can receive the potential intellect[128] and be completed by the actual intellect.

---

[125] Cf. 100.16-22 above.

[126] *hai koinai ennoiai* (103.38). In his inroduction Verbeke (1957) li-lii and Ballériaux 165-168 identify these with the Stoic common notions (on which see Todd [1973]). But the phrase refers to the same definitions and axioms as are identified in the next sentence. Cf. Themistius *In Analytica Posteriora* 6.32-7.3 for *koinai ennoiai* used to describe *axiômata*, and see Todd (1973) 62 note 85 for other examples of this association in later Greek philosophy.

[127] That teaching and learning require preestablished knowledge is an Aristotelian commonplace; cf. *Metaphysics* 6.2, 1027a20-22, *Ethica Nicomachea* 6.3, 1139b26-27, and *Analytica Posteriora* 1.1, 71a1-2 (cf. Themistius 2.5-25 *ad loc.*). Themistius is trying to integrate this principle into the Aristotelian noetic.

[128] Cf. 97.31-33 and 98.34-35 above.

104.14: And the inquiry pursued by some [thinkers], more recent as well as older ones, into whether all *souls* are one,[129] would be better directed into whether all *intellects* are one. For while the soul may according to them be one and separate, still its faculties are many, and plainly different from one another (i.e., the nutritive faculty from the faculty of perception, and the latter from the faculty of desire). But in the case of the intellect, and above all the theoretical intellect, the inquiry [into whether all intellects are one] is a necessary consequence for those who accept that in its case its essence is the same as its activity. For when one person teaches and another learns, either they do not think the same things, or if they do think the same things, then they have the same activity, and therefore also the [same] essence.

<The three intellects:
passive, potential, and productive>

*<*The distinction between perception
and the potential intellect*>*

104.23: But if the faculty of perception does not share in the imperishability of light (cf. 103.24-26), then neither does the potential intellect share in the imperishability of the productive intellect.[130] Yet even if perception is much more unaffected [by the body] than are its organs, and is not affected along with them ("for if," he says [1.4, 408b21-22], "an old man acquired an appropriate eye, he would have just the same vision as a youth"), it is still not entirely unaffected but somehow shares in the affection along with the organs. The [potential] intellect, on the other hand, is entirely[131] unaffected and separate.

---

[129] This is the title of Plotinus 4.9 [8].

[130] This sentence presents an aporia to which the next sentence, introduced by the particle *ê* (cf. note 120), offers the reply. The aporia is extracted from one arm of the dilemma regarding the unity of the intellect constructed at 103.21-26. The transition here is, however, unusually abrupt, even for this excursus.

[131] "Entirely" (*pantapasin*), repeated at 105.11 below, is Themistius' addition, crucial for his distinction (at 105.13-34) between the potential and

104.29: And this is clear from what he said earlier, while he was still discussing the potential intellect and had not yet mentioned the productive intellect. He says:

"That the faculties of perception and thought are not similarly unaffected is clear from the organs of perception and from perception [itself]. Perception, that is, cannot go on perceiving after an intense object of perception, e.g., low sounds after loud sound, or indistinct smells and colours after intense colours and smells. [*105*] But when the intellect thinks an[132] 'intense' object of thought, it thinks inferior things not less but even more. The faculty of perception, that is, is not unaccompanied by the body, whereas [the intellect] is separate" (429a29-429b5).

These are distinctions, that is, that are drawn with direct reference to the potential intellect; for to it belongs the transition [from superior to inferior things].[133] And a little earlier [he says]: "It is not reasonable, then, that [this intellect] be mixed with body, ... nor that it have an organ as does the faculty of perception" (429a24-26). And a little earlier still: "the faculty of thinking must, therefore, be unaffected but capable of receiving the form" (429a15-16).

105.8: Thus he is clearly of the view that while perception is less easily affected than the organs (those of perception, that is), it is neither entirely unaffected nor separate, whereas the potential

---

common intellects. At *De Anima* 3.4, 429b5 it seemed that the separation of the potential intellect "from all body" (cf. Themistius 95.5) established it as a precondition for thinking, not as something "entirely" independent of the body. This strained interpretation of the text is the exegetical basis for Themistius' notion of the potential intellect as a component in an eternal noetic compound (cf. 108.32-34).

[132] Heinze's addition of *ti* here (105.2) is unnecessary given that this quotation differs elsewhere from the received Aristotelian text at 104.34-105.1. I have not recorded these differences since they do not alter the essential meaning; cf. Heinze's apparatus for details.

[133] This reference to the immediate context seems to be the best construction to place on the very elliptical sentence *hê - toutou* (105.5). Others take it as having a more general reference: "il doit donc passer d'un concept à l'autre" (Balfériaux); "perché di questo e proprio il passagio discorsivo" (De Falco).

intellect, insofar as it does not employ a bodily organ for its activity, is entirely unmixed with the body, unaffected, and separate.

<The distinction between the
potential and common intellects>

105.13: But if the potential intellect is like this, what next would he describe as the intellect that is passive and perishable? This is what we were proposing to consider,[134] and the simplest way to do so would be to enlist ARISTOTLE as our partner. So let us see again[135] what he says in pursuing the problem of the intellect in his preliminary discussion in Book One. If the philosopher's texts are repeatedly rubbed like tinder, his thought might flash forth![136]

105.18: "But discursive reasoning, and loving or hating, are not affections of that thing [the productive intellect], but of this thing that has it, insofar as it has it. Thus, when this too is destroyed, it [the productive intellect] neither remembers nor loves. For these did not belong to it, but to the common [intellect] that has perished" (1.4, 408b25-29).

He could, therefore, be saying that the common [intellect] is the passive and perishable one. Yet regarding the potential intellect at least he explicitly says that it must be unaffected, separate, and "capable of receiving the form, and potentially such [as it] but not [identical with] it" (429a15-16), and that it not be mixed with the body (429a24-25), nor have a bodily organ (429a26), and that it and perception not be unaffected in the same way (429a29-30).

105.26: So if his claims about this intellect are not inconsistent, then according to him the common and potential intellects must be distinct. And while the common intellect is perishable, passive and inseparable from and mixed with the body, the potential

---

[134] Cf. 101.5-6 above.
[135] Cf. above 101.19-23.
[136] Cf. Plato *Republic* 4, 435a1-2 for this simile.

intellect is unaffected, unmixed with the body and separate (for he says this of it explicitly).[137] It is like a forerunner of the productive intellect, as the [sun's] ray is of the daylight,[138] or as the flower is a forerunner of the fruit. For in other cases too nature does not immediately provide the final state without a prelude; instead, things that are deficient, but of the same kind as more complete things, are the latter's forerunners.

<The distinction between the
potential and productive intellects>

105.34: The potential intellect, then, is itself separate, unmixed, and unaffected (for he says this of it in his own words), yet it is not separate in the same way as the productive intellect. See again [*106*] what he says about the productive intellect in comparing it with the potential intellect:

> "And one intellect is like this by becoming all things, the other by producing all things, like a positive state such as light; for in a way light too makes potential colours actual colours. And this intellect is separate, unaffected, and unmixed, being in essence activity. For that which produces [an affection] is always more estimable than that which is affected, and the first principle than the matter" (430a14-19).

Just as if we were to describe the sun too as more separate than its ray![139]

106.7: Thus he clearly believes that *both* intellects are separate, but that the productive intellect is more separate, more unaffected and more unmixed, and that while the potential intellect is prior in time in its presence in us, the actual intellect is prior in nature,

---

[137] Cf. note 131 above.

[138] The langauge of "precursive (or forerunning) illuminations" (*prodromoi ellampseis*) can be found at Plotinus 6.7 [38].7.12.

[139] At 103.32-34 above the productive intellect is represented as illuminating the potential intellect in the individual soul. Here, however, the potential intellect is itself part of the source of illumination; its status as a ray from the sun indicates the intimacy of that relation, and reinforces the dubious distinction between the potential and passive intellects drawn just above.

i.e., in completeness.[140] Indeed he believes that the potential intellect does not even have priority in time, but that while it may be prior in its presence in me or you, it is not prior without qualification, as neither is the forerunner to the king, nor the [sun's] ray to the daylight, nor the flower to the fruit.[141]

<Corroboration from Plato>

106.14: [ARISTOTLE] describes as perishable the common intellect in respect of which a human being is that which is compounded from soul and body, [a compound] in which there are emotions and appetites.[142] That PLATO also takes these [passions][143] to be perishable is clear from what is said in the *Timaeus*:

> *106.17*: "When they had taken over an immortal principle of soul, they next fashioned for it a mortal body by framing a globe around, building on another kind of soul that was mortal, and that had in itself terrible and necessary passions: first, pleasure, the strongest lure of evil; next, pains that flee from good; and also boldness and fear, two foolish counsellors; anger hard to entreat, and hope too easily led astray. These they blended together with irrational sense and desire that shrinks from no venture, and so compounded the mortal part of the soul. And in awe of polluting the divine part on account of all these, except insofar as was altogether necessary, they housed the mortal part apart from it, building between head

---

[140]   *teleiotêti*, i.e., in actuality; see note 44. Cf. also 99.30-32. Here as earlier (98.12-19) Themistius regards the priority of the actual intellect as corresponding to the order of nature (cf. note 43).

[141]   Ballériaux 217, compares the first two of these metaphors with, respectively, Plotinus 5.1 [10].6.28-30 and 5.5 [32].3.8-13, but rather exaggerates their significance in the present passage which is dominated by Aristotelian concepts.

[142]   Cf. *De Anima* 1.1, 403a 3-25 where the passions (*pathê*) are described as "common" (*koina*) to the soul and body; cf. *koina* at 403a4 with Themistius *In De Anima* 7.1, 8-9. This shows more clearly than the earlier discussion that what "common" means for Themistius in the phrase "common intellect" is this link between soul and body.

[143]   *pathê* is translated as "passions" to bring out the link that Themistius sees between them and the "passive" (*pathêtikos*) intellect; "emotions" is employed for *thumoi*.

and breast, as an isthmus and boundary, the neck, which they placed between to keep the two apart. In the breast, then, and the trunk (as it is called) they fastened the mortal kind of soul" (*Timaeus* 69c5-e4).[144]

And in a general summary of what he has said about the soul he writes: "Concerning the soul, then, so much is mortal, and so much divine" (*Timaeus* 72d4).

106.29: And most of the weightiest arguments for the immortality of the soul that [PLATO] investigated refer essentially to the intellect: (1) the one based on self-motion (it was shown, that is, that only the intellect was self-moved, if we could think of movement in place of activity);[145] [*107*] (2) the one that takes learning to be recollection;[146] and (3) the one on the similarity to God.[147] It would also not be difficult to associate with the intellect those of his other arguments thought particularly credible, as also the more credible of those elaborated by ARISTOTLE himself in the *Eudemus*.[148]

107.4: From these it is clear that PLATO too believes that while the [productive] intellect is "alone immortal" (430a23), though also itself some [aspect] of the soul,[149] the passions and the reason present in them (which ARISTOTLE calls "passive intellect") are perishable. The passions of the human soul, that is, are not entirely irrational in that they at least obey reason[150] and are

---

[144] This is based partly on Cornford's translation. Themistius deviates slightly from the received Platonic text; see Heinze's apparatus. The major omission is 69c7, a reference to the body serving as a vehicle (*ochêma*). That may have been thought irrelevant in the present context; elsewhere Themistius does refer to the Neoplatonic doctrine of the "luminous vehicle" of the soul; cf. *In De Anima* 19.33-34. Cf. also *ibid* 11.14-16 for a general reference to this passage of the *Timaeus*.

[145] Cf. *Phaedrus* 245c5-246a2.

[146] Cf. *Phaedo* 72e3-77a5.

[147] Cf. *Theaetetus* 176b1-3.

[148] 106.29-107.5 = Aristotle Frag. 38 Rose.³

[149] Cf. 103.15-18 above where the same inference is made as part of the general argument for the productive intellect not being the first God.

[150] *hupakouei* (107.8). Cf. Plato *Republic* 4, 441e6 and *Timaeus*. 70b8, and Aristotle *Ethica Nicomachea* 8.6, 1149a25-26.

trained and admonished; but while the passions of irrational
animals entirely fail to comprehend reason, or in some cases
barely reveal a dim trace of it, those in the human soul are
combined with reason. Boldness, fear and hope, that is, directly
reveal that they are in the rational soul, for they extend into the
future.[151] Hence they do not exist in irrational animals, but only
pleasure and pain at what is pleasant and painful in the present,
and these passions are entirely insensitive to reason and intellect.
In human beings this is <not> so, but[152] their passions too share
in reason in such a way that when moderated they become virtues.
This is a sign that it is not their nature but their lack of
moderation that is irrational. And it was not wrong for ZENO and
his school to hold the passions of the human soul to be "per-
versions of reason," i.e., mistaken judgments of reason.[153]

107.18: And the passive intellect and rational passion (i.e., the
passion of the human soul) could be described as identical, and
because of the intellect being housed[154] in the body these [pas-
sions] come to share in, and pay heed to, reason; for the intellect
could only be housed in the body through being fastened together,[155] i.e., in contact, with it through the passions as intermediar-
ies. As the divine PLATO says, "it is unlawful for the impure to be
in contact with the pure" (*Phaedo* 67b2). Therefore "when they
had taken over an immortal principle of soul," he says, "they next
fashioned for it a mortal body by framing a globe around"
(*Timaeus* 69c5-6). But that this might be possible, and an
immortal principle be "housed" in the body, "they weaved," he
says, "another type of soul with it, mortal and destined to die."[156]

---

[151] Cf. 109.18-27 (on *De Anima* 430a31-430b1) below on intellect adding
the thought of time to the data of perception and imagination.

[152] For *de houtôs ara* (107.15) read Browne's proposal *de <ouch> houtôs
alla* in light of the Arabic translation.

[153] 107.17-18 = Von Arnim, SVF 1.208.

[154] For the metaphor see *Timaeus* 69c8 and 69d7 (= 106.18, 24 above).

[155] On this language cf. *Timaeus* 69e4 and 73b3-4, and also 98.27 above
with note 48.

[156] This blends *Timaeus* 41d1-2 with 69c6-7. The term "destined to die"
(*epikêros*, 107.27) is not, however, in the text of the *Timaeus*. The phrase

For the bond joining the immortal with the mortal had itself to be mortal too; for when the mortal perishes, its bond with the immortal perishes along with it.[157]

<Corroboration from Theophrastus[158]>

107.30: It is also valuable to quote THEOPHRASTUS' account of the potential and actual intellects.

107.31:[159] On the potential intellect, then, he says the following:

"How can the [potential] intellect, being from without and as if added, still be innate [to the soul]? And what is its nature? That it is in actuality nothing, but in potentiality all things, in just the same way as perception, is correct. It must not, that is, be interpreted as being itself nothing[160] (for that would be captious), but as some underlying potentiality, in just the same way as with material [bodies]. But 'from outside' is not, then, to be understood as 'added,' but as 'being encompassed in the first generation [of the embryo]'." [*108*]

108.1[161] "How can [the potential intellect] become the objects of thought, and what is it to be affected <by> them? For this must be so if [the potential intellect] is going to come to actuality just as perception does. But what affection is there for an incorporeal

"another type of soul" (*allo eidos psuchês*) recalls Themistius' use of *De Anima* 2.2, 413b24-27 at 102.11-13 and 103.7-9 above; there Aristotle speaks of the theoretical intellect as "another kind of soul" (413b26).

[157] This sentence is based on *Timaeus* 42e7-43a6.

[158] The fragments from Theophrastus in this section will be cited from the edition at Barbotin, 248-273; this should be consulted for information on similar quotations in Priscian *Metaphrasis in Theophrastum* (SA 1.2). They are also edited by Hicks, in his edition of the *De Anima* 589-596. Emendations in light of the Arabic translation point up the uncertainty surrounding the text of these fragments. For some discussion of Themistius' paraphrase in the medieval transmission of evidence on the Theophrastean noetic see Huby.

[159] 107.31-108.1 = Barbotin, Frag. Ia.

[160] For *oude* (107.34) read *ouden* in light of the Arabic translation (cf. Browne), a change that reflects 107.33, as Browne notes, as well as 108.7.

[161] 108.1-6 = Barbotin, Frag. Ib, and 108.6-7 = Frag. Ic. At 108.3 I follow Barbotin in reading *asomatou* for *somatos*; cf. his discussion at 280-282. Heinze offered this as a conjecture, and it was accepted by Hicks 590.

through the action of an incorporeal? What kind of change [is this]? And is the source [of the change] derived from the [object] or from the [intellect]? Because [the intellect] is affected it would seem to be from [the object] (for nothing that is affected is so from itself). Yet because [the intellect] is the source of all things, and thinking is in its power, unlike the senses,[162] [the source of the change would seem to be] from it. But perhaps this too would seem absurd if the [potential] intellect has the nature of matter by being [in actuality] nothing, yet potentially all things."

108.8: It would prolong this to quote the next part too, although it is not stated at length, but in fact in too compressed and brief a way, in style at least. For in relation to its material it is crammed with numerous problems, reflections and solutions. These are in Book Five of his *Physics*, and Book Two of his *On the Soul*, from all of which it is clear that they too [ARISTOTLE and THEOPHRAS-TUS] pursue essentially the same problems regarding the potential intellect [as I have],[163] [viz.] whether it is from without or innate, and they try to define it as being in one way from without, but in another innate.

108.14:[164] They say that it too [the potential intellect] is unaffected and separate, just like the intellect that is productive and actual.[165] "For this intellect," he says, "is unaffected, unless it is

---

[162] This translation follows the punctuation adopted by Hicks and Barbotin, and relies on a similar contrast between thought and sense perception at *De Anima* 2.5, 417b24-26. (Heinze's punctuation would destroy that contrast by having the text say that "thinking and not thinking is in [the intellect's] power, as with the senses.") Even so, the text followed here does contain the rather awkward Greek clause (*kai mê hôsper tais aisthêsesin* (108.6). De Falco's (unexplained) procedure of omitting *hôsper–aisthêsesin* altogether is therefore attractive, and does have the Themistian parallel at 111.29-30 where the potential intellect is said to be able to think and not to think.

[163] This supplement seems justified (1) in light of Themistius' quotation from Theophrastus in the context of his discussion at 102.24-29 above, and (2) in view of the claims made at 106.7-14 where the potential intellect is seen as an external intellect that precedes the actual intellect in the soul. Themistius may well see 107.35-108.1 above as confirmation of the latter view.

[164] 108.14-18; cf. Barbotin, Frag. IV b.

[165] Cf. 105.34-106.14, where there is the qualification that the potential intellect has these properties to a lesser degree.

passive in some other way." And [he says] that in its case "being passive" must not be understood as "being moveable" (for movement is incomplete), but as activity.[166] And he goes on to say that while there are no perceptions without body, the [potential] intellect is separate [from body].[167]

108.18:[168] In also touching on the distinctions drawn by ARIS-TOTLE regarding the productive intellect he says:

> "What must be considered is our saying (430a10-12) that in the whole of nature one thing is like matter, and is in potentiality, while another is causative and productive; and that 'that which produces [an affection] is always more estimable than that which is affected, and the first principle than the matter'" (430a18-19).

While accepting this, he still pursues problems:

> "What, then, are these two natures? And what, furthermore, is that which is substrate for, and dependent on, the productive intellect? For the intellect is somehow mixed out of that which is productive and that which is potential. So if the [intellect] that moves[169] is innate [to the soul], it would also have [to be so] originally and perpetually. But if a later [development], with what, and how, does it come into existence? It seems that if indeed it is also imperishable, it is a substance[170] that does not come into existence. If in that

---

[166] Cf. Aristotle *Physics* 3.2, 201b31-32 for the general principle. At 112.25-33 below, in an expansive paraphrase of *De Anima* 3.7, 431a4-7, Themistius explores the same principle in contrasting perception and the intellect.

[167] Cf. *De Anima* 3.4, 429b4-5, and Themistius 95.4-5 *ad loc.*

[168] 108.22-28 = Barbotin, Frag. XII, where the context (108.18-22) is added. Cf. the closely related citation at 102.24-29 above, with Barbotin 286-288.

[169] Cf. 103.2 above for this use of *kinein* ("move") of the productive intellect.

[170] For *d'oun hôs* (108.26) read *d'ousia*, proposed by Browne on the basis of the Arabic translation; this variant is apparently not in the Arabic in the earlier version of this passage at 102.28. It is certainly a desirable part of *Themistius'* text since he subsequently (108.32-34) reads Theophrastus as proposing that the actual and potential intellects are a separate compound related as form to matter. Whether it was part of Theophratus' text is another question. See also Themistius *In De Anima* 49.9 for the theoretical intellect spoken of as an *ousia*.

case it is inherent [to the soul], why is it not so always? Why is there loss of memory, confusion and falsity? Is it because of the mixture [with the passive intellect]?"[171]

108.28: From all this it is clear that our basic interpretation[172] is not mistaken: that for [THEOPHRASTUS and ARISTOTLE] there is (1) one intellect that is the passive and perishable one, that they also call "common" and "inseparable from the body," (and it is because of mixture with *this* [intellect] that THEOPHRASTUS says that loss of memory and confusion occur [for the productive intellect]);[173] and (2) another that is the intellect that is as though compounded from the potential and actual [intellects], and this they posit as separate from the body, imperishable, and not coming into existence.[174] And these intellects are in one way two natures, yet in another one, for that [which is compounded] from matter and form is one.[175]

[171] Cf. note 108. The reference to the passive intellect is supplied to bring out Themistius' reading of this passage.

[172] *huponoumen* (108.29). The verb is used elsewhere to characterize allegorical intepretation. Its presence here suggests some acknowledgement on Themistius' part that his interpretation is what a modern scholar might call a reconstruction.

[173] But the mixture envisaged by Theophrastus at 108.24-28 must be that of the productive and *potential* intellects (cf. Hicks in his edition of the *De Anima* 595 and Barbotin 161-172). At 108.28 *mixis* ("mixture"), that is, must echo the earlier reference (108.24) to the intellect being "somehow mixed from the productive and potential intellects." The introduction of the passive intellect here is scarcely justified.

[174] This is the clearest definition of the contrast, developed exegetically at 104.23-106.14 above, between the actual (or productive) and potential intellects on the one hand, and the passive intellect on the other. It is regrettable that it is not systematically linked with other themes introduced in the excursus such as the notion that we are the productive intellect, and that that intellect is a type of soul (cf. note 115).

[175] Cf. 99.17-18. We can now see why Themistius, unlike Alexander (cf. note 14) and the author of the *De Intellectu*, did not use the notion of a material intellect in his analysis of the development of the potential intellect at 95.9-21. For him the potential intellect is material only in its special status as the eternal matter of the actual intellect, and is not inseparable from the body. Contrast Alexander *De Anima* 90.14-16. Ibn Rushd did, however, refer to the Themistian potential intellect as the material intellect; see the passage from his commentary on *Metaphysics* 12 (*Lambda*) at Genequand 104. See also Hyman 176-180 on Ibn Rushd's reception of this evidence.

<Conclusion>

108.35: But, as I have said, demonstrating the opinion of philosophers involves special study and reflection. Still, it does seem perhaps relevant to assert [*109*] that someone could most effectively grasp the insight of ARISTOTLE and THEOPHRASTUS into these matters, indeed perhaps also that of PLATO himself, from the statements that we have gathered.

<PARAPHRASE OF 3.6>

109.4 (430a26-31): So when this potential intellect acquires its own form through the productive intellect illuminating it,[176] it first thinks the uncombined and undivided things that are signified (the ones distinguished in the categories), in which there is not yet truth and falsity. But as it progresses[177] it also combines them with one another (e.g., "Socrates" with "walks"), and in these truth and falsity is indeed present. And it does not combine them like a heap, but so as to make the many one again, and to embrace in one act of thought the plurality of uncombined things that are signified. "Socrates does philosophy," that is, is like this, and this combination of thoughts resembles the combination of limbs in EMPEDOCLES[178] by which Love, for him, combines the scattered limbs of animals. And just as for him not every combination of limbs produces an animal, so neither in this case does every combination [produce] truth, but one type produces truth, another falsity (e.g., the combination of the incommensurable with the diagonal produces truth, but that of the commensurable

---

[176] Only here does Themistius link the hylomorphic relation between the productive and potential intellects (99.17-18; 100.31; 108.32-34) with the model of illumination used at 103.32-33.

[177] Cf., however, 112.14-24 below where thinking the essences of uncombined things (especially those of immaterial forms) is recommended as epistemically more reliable; such thinking is, however, possible only after the discursive thinking described here has occurred.

[178] Cf. Diels-Kranz 31B57.

falsity). And just as in his case the animal duly emerges uncombined out of uncombined limbs, so does the statement duly emerge uncombined out of uncombined things that are signified.[179]

109.18 (430a31-430b1): The intellect also adds the thought of time to many things when it thinks about them as past or as future, and comprehending time too either as past or future is a quite distinctive property of the intellect (i.e., the faculty superior to the imagination). Perception and imagination, that is, are entirely unable to apprehend time, and above all past or future time; no image or perception, that is, of someone who has done philosophy, or who has run, comes to exist in the soul, as though there is not even a likeness [of them]. Instead each of these moves perception or imagination by being directly present, and it is for the intellect to add the thought of time. Truth and falsity also apply to time; for while "Croesus the Lydian lived" is true, "Croesus the Lydian is alive" is a falsehood.

109.27 (430b1-6): Now [the intellect] often combines what belongs to the object as belonging to it (when it says "Snow is white"), and often what belongs as not belonging (when it says "Snow is not white"). In the latter case, that is, it combines one type of thing with another so that it does not belong [to it]. And for someone to call such cases division rather than combination would not be incorrect, as denial does resemble division and assertion combination. But perhaps they are also all divisions, in that the intellect divides what the imagination received from perception in a confused way. The imagination, that is, has an image of Socrates walking as a unity, whereas the intellect divides into separate [units] "Socrates" and "walks," and gives a separate report about things that are not separate. Yet after separating them, it again makes them one; i.e., "Socrates does philosophy" is one statement as well as one thought, [*110*] and truth and falsity belong to it as to one statement. There are, then, these two

---

[179] Cf. 116.17-19 below (on 432a12-14) where Socrates is given as an example of an uncombined thought.

distinct properties of the intellect: the ability to group together many thoughts into an apparent unity, and the addition of the thought of time. Neither of them is a function of the imagination or of perception.

110.5 (430b6-14): The uncombined and undivided is spoken of in two ways: i.e., either (1) where a thing is neither divided in potentiality nor in actuality (as is the case with the immaterial forms,[180] and the point), or (2) where it is divided in potentiality but undivided in actuality (as with the line, and magnitude generally). Now both the intellect and the time of which it makes additional use in the act of thinking are, like these, both divided and undivided. In the case of the immaterial forms both time and the intellect itself are completely undivided, but where the intellect thinks things that are divided in potentiality but undivided in actuality [case (2)], it thinks [them] by being itself undivided in actuality, and in undivided time. That is, it thinks length as one thing, and not this [half] in one half of the time, and that [half] in the other; in that way it would think two lengths and not length, and by dividing length into lengths it would also divide time.

110.15 (430b14-15):[181] Take (3) that which is undivided not in quantity but in species, e.g., man or Socrates. For both are undivided in species, in that neither is the thought of man divided in species, yet, assuming [this] for individuals, neither indeed is the thought of Socrates. Now the intellect thinks these things that are undivided in species both in undivided time and by undivided thinking. It does not, in other words, think one half of Socrates in half [the time], and the other half in the other half! Nor is the combination involved in the thought extended along with the process of the utterance through which we express "man." In fact,

---

[180] This is Themistius' example; on the role of immaterial forms in thinking cf. below 112.23-24, and 114.31-115.9.

[181] 110.15-111.7 was loosely translated by John Philoponus in his commentary on *De Anima* 3.4-8, a work extant only in William of Moerbeke's translation; cf. 78.14-80.54 ed. Verbeke (1966).

it is just this that is one of the miracles of the intellect: while it hears in time it thinks not in time, but in the now[182] that is either not time at all, or is partless time. And it itself thinks by an act of thinking that is partless, since it is not, as I said, extended along with the word [uttered], nor does it add part of the thought with part of the word, i.e., with each syllable, but while the word is divided, the thought is undivided.

110.27 (430b16-20): Were someone to contend that the thought too is divided, he could call it divided accidentally and not divided in itself, but [just] insofar as the word and voice through which the intellect both expresses [the word] and thinks [are divided], and insofar as [the thought], though partless, is in a way that is hard to describe adapted to the voice, despite the latter's having parts. And many things are divided accidentally, and not divided in themselves, but [only] insofar as the things by which they become known [are divided]. For in this way we might describe as accidentally divided even the limit of the time in which [the intellect] thinks, because it is an accident of the time of which it is a limit, and becomes known by means of time.[183] For unless the year that is now, and the month, day and hour completed the now *in extenso*, we would not even conceive of the partless now. The reason is that in everything that is divided there is also something undivided (just as there is something uncombined in all compounds), and while this may not be separate from them or be capable of existing in itself, it is [*111*] still present in them. For neither can what is signified be distinguished from the voice that signifies, yet without a voice it is not even possible to make an utterance, and perhaps [someone] cannot gain understanding by himself without also adjusting [his voice] to

---

[182]   *to nun* (110.23). This could be translated "the instant" ('l'instante', De Falco), but it is better to render it literally as a technical term for the concept introduced and explained by Aristotle at *Physics* 4.11 and 13.

[183]   He is referring to the now; cf. Aristotle *Physics* 4.11, 220a21-22 and 4.13, 222a18-19 for the now as the limit between before and after, and as accidentally time.

himself by some utterance. But all the same this is what makes the utterance partless although it has parts, and undivided although it is divided. In the same way the undivided is also present in time, in length, and in absolutely everything that is continuous, and it makes length one and time one, for what is continuous is also what is one. That is why we call the stadium one, and the day one and the month one. This is what I say is undivided and uncompounded in length and time, despite the latter being divided and being compounded. Otherwise all quantities would be divided, and all be a plurality, though in fact even plurality is encompassed by unity, and not only continuous quantity but indeed also that which is divided. That is, a set of two, three, and ten [things] is a plurality encompassed by unity.

111.13 (430b20-23): And when I say that the point and the now are undivided, they must be understood as undivided and uncompounded in a different way, i.e., as if the undivided exists [for them] by nature and in itself. That is because they are undivided through the privation of extension. Certainly the intellect thinks and defines them in this way – not, that is, by encountering them [directly] (for it does not even have a shape of its own),[184] but by removing the [temporal] interval and [spatial] quantity of which they are limits. For the intellect, just as for perception, that is, some things are objects of thought by a [direct] encounter[185] where it also grasps their nature,[186] others so by privation and abstraction. For just as for perception white and light exist by a [direct] encounter, and black and darkness by privation (and for hearing noise exists by a [direct] encounter, silence by privation),

---

[184] It is, in other words, the potential intellect; cf. *De Anima* 3.4, 429a18-22, with Themistius 94.18-27.

[185] *kat'epibolên* (111.19). The term *epibolê* ("[direct] encounter") may have its origins in Epicurean epistemology, but it and the verb *epiballein* (translated "encounter directly" at 111.17) are regularly used in later Greek philosophy to describe both perceptual and mental awareness.

[186] Following Heinze's suggestion of *drattomenôi* (sc. *nôi*) for the *drattomena* of the manuscripts. This rare verb is probably another Platonic metaphor; cf. *Lysis* 209e5, its only use in the Platonic corpus.

so too for the intellect the good exists by a [direct] encounter, the bad by privation. And this could be the Platonic saying about matter, that "it is to be grasped by bastard reasoning" (*Timaeus* 52b2), for it is precisely a "bastard" activity of both the intellect and perception that occurs, not through the [direct] impact[187] of form but through a withdrawal.

111.26 (430b23-24): Now if perception did not have a potentiality both for being both active and for being inactive but was always active, it would never perceive darkness, nor would hearing perceive silence. Similarly, unless there were also an intellect naturally disposed to both, i.e., to thinking and to inactivity (or better, both to thinking and to non-thinking), it would not think evil things, nor think that which is without shape and form. Now the potential intellect is like this, for it is somehow through contraries that it becomes acquainted with contraries (the forms through being active, the [things thought] by privation through its potentiality); that is because potentiality and actuality are in a way contraries.

111.34 (430b24-26):[188] So if there is an intellect that does not share in potentiality, then neither does it think privations, nor, therefore, evil things.[189] Both the intellect from without[190] is like

---

[187] *kat'epereisin* (111.26). In contrast with *epibolê* which defines the act of mental attention, this term picks out the effect of an object of perception on a perceiver. It may have its origins in the Stoic theory of vision; cf. the Alexandrian *Mantissa* (sA 2.1) 130.22, 26, 30; 131.22.

[188] Themistius' interpretation of these lines is also found in modern commentators. It has been challenged by Berti 146, who lists its adherents (at note 28). He argues that Aristotle is only identifying the intellection of things that have no contrary, and not the activity of a subject, God, who knows himself.

[189] Cf. Aristotle *Metaphysics* 9.9, 1051a17-21 for this claim made for eternal things.

[190] De Falco's translation of 111.35-112.1 proceeds as though the intellect identified here as "from without" (i.e., the productive intellect) is the subject of the sentence that follows. He goes on to interpret *houtos* (112.1) and *autou* (112.7) as referring to it. But quite apart from Aristotelian parallels suggesting that it is the divine intellect that is being described in what follows, the particles *te ... kai* 111.35 ensure that the "First Cause" (112.1) is a distinct entity and not a complementary description of the intellect "from without."

this, and much more so [*112*] the First Cause by its still greater removal from potentiality.[191] For this is why this [intellect *qua* First Cause] thinks that which is most fully, i.e., that which is most fully form[192] and furthest from privation and formlessness. And because it is itself like this, it thinks itself, and it is this whose essence it is proper to describe as activity, and as [itself] separate in an exact sense, i.e., as not adapted in the slightest to potentiality. But this is not[193] why intellect of this sort is more estimable than one that thinks contraries; for a more estimable intellect is not one that thinks more things, but one that thinks better things.[194] And in its case the object of thought and the intellect are not divided [from one another], as with the potential intellect, but it is an object of thought insofar as it is intellect, and also again intellect insofar as it is object of thought.

112.8 (430b26-27): And truth in its case is without qualification; indeed it is itself truth, as it does not express truth by thinking something else but by thinking itself. Our intellect, on the other hand, insofar as it has a slight resemblance[195] to that intellect, does not also display truth without qualification, but [only] as what is contrary to falsity. For if truth lies in assertion, falsity must

---

[191] In other words, greater than the actual intellect that actualizes the potential intellect of which it is the form. It is not, therefore, strictly separate because it is adapted to potentiality, unlike the divine intellect as described at 112.4-5. On the first cause as being without potentiality cf. Aristotle *Metaphysics* 12 (*Lambda*).10, 1075b21-24.

[192] Cf. Aristotle *Metaphysics* 12 (*Lambda*).7, 1072b18-19.

[193] At 112.5 the second *ou* has been deleted.

[194] The divine intellect, that is, thinks only the less numerous immaterial forms; cf. below 114.34-35, and 115.3-4.

[195] *smikron indalma* (112.10). The term *indalma* is Plotinian (cf. e.g. *Enneads* 5.3 [49].8.48), but here used loosely. The potential intellect is illuminated only by the productive intellect (103.32-33, 109.4-5 above), and this intellect is not the First God (102.36-103.19), identified here as the "First Cause" (111.35-112.1); the "resemblance" between our intellect and the divine intellect is therefore a comparison rather than the expression of a metaphysical relation.

lie in denial, so that [our intellect] always has falsity confounded[196] with truth, and thought about along with it.

112.14 (430b27-30): When, however, [our intellect] examines one of the uncombined things that are signified,[197] and thinks about its form and the definition of its essence, it errs least, though it does not always light upon what is [true]. Instead like vision, which errs least in judging only the white thing, but errs frequently in asserting that the white thing is Cleon,[198] [our] intellect is also in most cases unerring and correct as long as it restricts itself to just the thought of the essence (e.g., to that of the good or of the fine). But when it says that one thing is good and another fine, it frequently makes the wrong assignment,[199] and transfers such qualities to things that are not of that sort,[200] and in just such cases there is considerable falsity and error. It ought, then, to restrict itself to the forms and above all seek out those without matter,[201] as the special function of the intellect concerns these.[202]

---

[196] *sumpephurmenon* (112.13; also 116.2 below), a Platonic metaphor (cf. *Phaedo* 66b5).

[197] Cf. 109.5-6 above.

[198] Cf. *De Anima* 3.3, 428b18-19, 21-22 for this contrast, drawn there between the special and incidental objects of perception. Themistius' claim that perception is "least prone to error" with regard to the special objects reflects 428b19; cf. also *De Anima* 2.6, 418a11-12 with Themistius 57.17-24. The latter passage shows that the commentator regarded the success of our perception of the special objects as dependent on empirical conditions; he does not, however, indicate how our intellect could err in thinking something's essence. For an Aristotelian answer cf. *Metaphysics* 9.10, 1051b25-33, and on the wider issues involved see Sorabji 139-142.

[199] *allotrionomei* (112.21), another Platonic metaphor; cf. *Theaetetus* 195a7 for its only Platonic use.

[200] Cf. 109.27-31 for examples of such combination and division. At *In De Anima* 30.24-34 Themistius contrasts such processes of discursive reasoning (*dianoeisthai*) with "thinking" (*noein*), there defined as insight into primary definitions.

[201] At 112.23 read *ta* for the first *to* in that line.

[202] Cf. 114.31-115.9 below on the capacity of the potential intellect to think immaterial forms.

<PARAPHRASE OF 3.7>

112.25 (431a4-7):[203] Yet even if the intellect is far better than the faculty of perception, most things belong to it analogously to perception. The activity of perception, that is, is not an affection, nor an alteration, nor even a movement at all; a movement, that is, involves what is incomplete, and what is always adding one thing after another, whereas the activity of perception is always complete,[204] and so it is not even a movement or another kind of movement. In the same way the encounter of the intellect with the objects of thought for someone who is already in a state of possessing [thoughts], just as with the knower's encounter[205] with the objects of knowledge, is not a movement but an activity, because it involves what is complete, and because it is itself complete. For [by contrast] the [actualization] of what is in potentiality is like a coming into existence rather than a completion.[206]

[203] Themistius omits comment on *De Anima* 431a1-3 (= 3.5, 430a19-21). It appears in his paraphrase of 3.5 (cf. 99.27-31, and 101.23-24), though whether it was also absent from the text that he used for 3.7 is uncertain; it was certainly known to other commentators (see Ross, Oxford Text, app. crit. *ad loc.*); cf. also Commentary on *De Intellectu* 108.3.

[204] Cf. *De Anima* 2.5, 417a14-20.

[205] Omitted is *energeia kai* (112.31) with the Arabic translation. Its presence would make the conclusion that such an encounter is not a movement but an activity (112.32) superfluous. Otherwise the Arabic translation is not followed. It has a negative at 112.30 corresponding to the *oude* that Heinze deleted and runs "so the mind's encounter with thoughts is not the activity of one to whom accrues the natural disposition, as you would say the scholar's encounter with data is not movement but activity" (trans. Browne). Browne proposes adding *energeia* after *ēdē* at 112.31. But the *hexis* at 112.30 is not really a natural disposition but the precondition for thinking exemplified by someone thoroughly acquainted with a body of knowledge and able to actualize it at will (cf. 95.9-32 above). The analogy between this condition and that actualized in perception is drawn at *De Anima* 2.5, 417a22-25 and 417b16-18. At 112.30-31 Themistius introduces it into his analogy between thinking and perceiving, and so *hôsper–epibolê* (112.31) is best read as a subordinate clause. In that way thinking and its illustration can be presented together as parallelling the case of perception (112.26-27) in being an activity and not a movement.

[206] This sentence is added to provide a contrast with the case of perception by recalling (from *De Anima* 2.5) the sense of potentiality that, in Aristotle's

112.33 (431a8-14): Certainly[207] in the following respect both
desire and avoidance are also analogous to [intellect and per-
ception].[208] [See] just above.[209] Perception, that is, sometimes
asserts only that a thing is yellow, at other times that the yellow
thing is also pleasant. So when perception asserts only that a
thing is [*113*] yellow, it neither avoids nor pursues it, but when
it adds the assertion that [the yellow thing] is pleasant (as with
honey), that is when it pursues it, and when [it adds] that it is
painful (as with bile), that is when it avoids it. Now observe just
the same thing in the case of the intellect too. When it thinks only
the essence of health, it neither avoids nor pursues it, but when
it adds the thought and judgment that health is good, that is when
it pursues it. Thus the good and the bad prevail on the intellect
in just the same way as the pleasant and the painful on perception.
Perception, that is, can apprehend neither the good nor the bad,
but only what produces pleasure or causes pain, whereas judging
the good and the bad belongs to the intellect alone, an intellect
which, as we have often said,[210] also adds in succession the
thought of time. But perception still believes that the pleasant and
the good, and the painful and the bad, are one, as it certainly
draws towards pleasant things and turns away from painful ones.
The intellect, on the other hand, frequently counteracts the
impulses of perception by saying that the pleasurable is something
different from the good, and the painful from the bad.

---

words, is "as we might speak of a boy being able to become a general"
(417b31-32). This is a "coming into existence" (*genesis*) rather than the
"completion" (*teleiôsis*) that would be involved in an adult becoming a general
(417b32); and it is the latter that Aristotle says the capacity for perception is
like (417b32-418a1).
   [207] Reading *goun* for *te oun* at 112.33.
   [208] This sentence seems to be Themistius' desperate attempt to provide some
transition between 431a4-7 and the unrelated discussion of practical reasoning
beginning at 431a8. "Intellect and perception" are supplied as the reference for
autois ("them") at 112.33, but the sentence is still awkward when *touto* (112.33)
has to be construed as a forward looking accusative of respect.
   [209] Cf. Aristotle *De Anima* 3.1, 425a30-425b4; the example of bile is used
there as here (113.2).
   [210] At 109.18-27.

113.14 (431a14-17): The purpose of images for the soul capable of discursive reasoning is just like that of sensations for perception, and the good and the bad serve the former[211] as the pleasant and the painful do the latter. So when [this soul] combines, for example, the image and the good, or the image and the bad, that is when it either avoids or pursues [something], pursuit resembling assertion, avoidance denial. But just as perception cannot be active without objects of perception, so neither can the intellect that is innate to our soul[212] be active without images derived from perception; indeed whenever the intellect desires or avoids, imagination in all cases precedes it. (But if there is some intellect neither so deficient that it desires, nor so weak that it avoids, *it* would not need imagination.)[213] And while desire associated with perception is appetite, desire associated with discursive reasoning is wishing, and while appetite is for the pleasant, wishing is for the good. And perception and perceptual desire [i.e., appetite] are identical in substrate, but different in definition, just as both intellect and wishing are identical in substrate, but different in essence. And the capacities for desire and avoidance are not distinct from one another, nor [jointly] distinct from the faculty of perception, as neither is that which wishes and that which does not wish distinct from one another, nor [jointly] distinct from the actual faculty of thinking. Instead, the same faculty is naturally disposed both to avoid and to pursue, as also both to wish and not wish, and these are all desires. For when perception avoids something, it *desires* avoidance, and when [the intellect] has a negative wish, it *desires* not to encounter what it does not wish.

113.32 (431b2-10):[214] We must now again take up something that we have often stated: that for the intellect the forms are in the

---

[211] At 113.15 read *têi de to agathon* for *to de agathon* , with the Arabic translation (cf. Browne).

[212] In other words, the potential intellect; cf. 98.34 for this language.

[213] This point is perhaps added to anticipate the later description (114.37-115.9) of the divine intellect as exclusively concerned with immaterial forms, though it would be equally true that the actual intellect does not need to think with the help of images.

[214] Themistius omits comment on 3.7, 431a17-431b1.

images (just as for perception they are in the sensations), and that the intellect thinks the forms in the images. The result for it, then, is that both in the presence and in the absence of perception it moves desire in just the same way. For it is the judgment that what it is thinking is good or bad that makes that thing something to be pursued or avoided. For on seeing a person [*114*] to be avoided, and realizing that they are hostile, it avoids them, yet even when it does not see them but presents itself with images and adds its judgment, it does the same thing.

114.2 (431b10-12): The preceding are the functions of the practical intellect; i.e., it is for it to move desire, since the theoretical intellect only becomes acquainted with things. It is, however, true that the pleasant and the painful are to perception, as truth and falsity are in turn to the theoretical intellect, with truth in the place of the good and falsity in that of the bad. The difference is that truth is true without qualification, and falsity similarly, whereas the good and the pleasant are [so] for somebody. The theoretical intellect, therefore, judges that which is without qualification [true], whereas the practical intellect judges that which is [so] for somebody.

114.9 (431b12-17): The intellect thinks things that are in themselves[215] objects of thought in a different way from the things spoken of by abstraction—I mean the line, the surface, and the whole matter of geometry. For while the latter are the limits of physical bodies, the intellect still thinks them without including physical body, just as though it could separate snubness from the nose or the flesh of which it is an accident. (In that case it would think that which cannot exist without the nose as existing without it!) But in fact the intellect cannot do this in the case of snubness, as the definition of snubness includes the nose; i.e., snubness is just hollowness of nose and flesh. But hollowness itself, and the curved, the straight, the bent, the triangular and the quadrilateral

---

[215] That is, the immaterial forms, the thinking of which is discussed at 114.31-115.9 below.

are things that the intellect can think about in and of themselves, although they do not exist in that way. The reason is that even if such things are not separate from physical bodies, still their definition and essence do not implicate matter. That, then, is why the intellect can render separate for itself things that are not in reality separate in order to think about quantity, and thinking about quantity does not require physical body, nor the affections belonging to it *qua* physical (e.g., heat, coldness, dryness, or moisture), but just its dimensions and limits. (And the reason why geometry and arithmetic are the sciences most detached from physical matter is that their demonstrations proceed without including it in their thinking. Hence they also need perception the least, because they also need matter the least. Astronomy and music may themselves aim for this, but they are not similarly successful; for them perception is instead both the beginning and end of their reasoning.)

114.31 (431b17-19): That, then, is how [the intellect] thinks abstract objects. But what must also be considered later, as well as discussed now, is whether, by being in the body and not separated from [physical] magnitude, it can also think the forms that are naturally separate and that are without qualification immaterial. It would, that is, seem plausible that just as that divine intellect, which is separate and exists in actuality, thinks none of the enmattered forms, neither does the enmattered intellect think any of the separate forms. It is reasonable that the divine intellect think none of the enmattered forms, as it has [*115*] no potentiality by which it can apprehend privations,[216] and this is not its inferiority but its superiority. For it does not have the potentiality for perishing either,[217] and it is not on that account made inferior in relation to things that do have it. So, to repeat, if this [divine intellect] thinks none of the enmattered forms,[218] it would seem

---

[216] Cf. 111.34-112.3 above.

[217] Cf. Aristotle *Metaphysics* 9.8, 1050b6-12 for the general connection between potentiality and perishability.

[218] This would mean, then, that it thinks only the separate immaterial forms; see also Themistius *In Metaphysica Lambda* 22.22-24. The productive intellect,

to follow that neither does the enmattered intellect think any of the forms that exist apart from matter. Yet this is not true, as this [enmattered intellect] has to the full the potentiality for thinking the immaterial forms too. For just as[219] it also thinks the enmattered forms by separating them from matter,[220] so is it clearly all the more naturally disposed to think the separate forms; for its inferiority in relation to the divine intellect is not that it can never think the immaterial forms, but that it cannot do so continuously and perpetually.[221]

<PARAPHRASE OF 3.8>

115.10 (431b20-24): Though the preceding [topics] deserve extended consideration, let us for now summarize what has been said about the soul by repeating that the soul is in a way all existing things; existing things, that is, are either objects of perception or objects of thought, and actual[222] knowledge is [identical with] the objects of knowledge, while actual perception is [identical with] the objects of perception. How this is so has also been adequately stated earlier,[223] but something else must still be added here.

---

by contrast, does seem to include enmattered forms in its intellection (cf. note 78). Themistius does, however, represent divine intellection in language similar to that used to characterize the thinking of this intellect at 100.7-10; cf. *In Metaphysica Lambda* 23.17-22, 32.14-33.6, and 33.24-26, and the Arabic passage translated by Pines (1987) 181-182. Presumably they have the same mode of comprehensive intellection despite the difference in range. Themistius' picture of divine intellection is thus more restricted than that proposed, for example, in a well known modern study; cf. Norman 67, who sees the Aristotelian God's self-thinking as "the same as ordinary human abstract thought."

[219] Reading *hôs* (suggested by the Arabic version) for *hos* at 115.6.

[220] Cf. above 98.1-2, and 100.1-3.

[221] Cf. 98.4-9 above where this contrast is drawn between the potential and (at least by implication) the actual intellects. Also cf. 94.10 regarding the former.

[222] *kat'energeian* (115.12). This is Themistius' qualification, omitted by Aristotle at 431b22-23.

[223] For knowledge cf. *De Anima* 3.4, 430a4-5, and for perception 2.5, 418a3-6.

115.15 (431b24-432a2): Now some things that exist are in potentiality, others in actuality, and by this token the soul too is in potentiality some forms, in actuality others. When it has the state of possessing perception and intellect,[224] but is not active, it is in potentiality existing things, but when it is active through both states, it is in actuality existing things. And we are right to say that the soul is all existing things since existing things are the forms, and each thing is what it is with respect to its form, while the matter is by contrast the cause of generation, i.e., of coming into existence, not of being. The incessant flux of bodies, that is, is because of the matter, whereas each thing is stable (i.e., the same for some time) because of the form. It is correct, therefore, to say that the soul is all existing things since it receives the forms of all existing things through both the intellect and perception, and becomes identical with them. (Not that it becomes identical with things in their totality; i.e., there is no stone in the soul, nor fire, nor earth!). What remains, then, is that the soul becomes the forms, and nothing prevents definition fitting together with definition, and form with form. Thus the soul is like the hand, in that the hand is "a tool of tools" (432a2) through which we use the other tools, and the soul[225] "a form of forms" (432a2) by which we apprehend the other forms. (Perhaps the soul is correctly said to be existing things not only because it receives all the forms, but also because it imposes the forms on matter.[226] It is, after all, the thing that shapes matter with various shapes, the life from it being much more striking[227] in the case of animals, while more indistinct in the case of plants and the elements.)

---

[224] Here (115.17) and at 115.24 below *nous* (intellect) is the receptive intellect *qua* state of possession described at 95.9-32.

[225] Aristotle (432a2-3) in fact says that the *intellect* is "form of forms" and perception "form of the objects of perception." Themistius conflates the two faculties into the single term "soul." Cf. 100.33 above for the productive intellect as "form of forms" in a description of the hierarchy of the faculties.

[226] Cf. above 98.27-28 where the same expression is used to describe the activity of a craft.

[227] At 115.33 *hê* is deleted as well as the gloss *tês hulês* deleted by Heinze.

115.35 (432a3-10): It follows that those who believe that there is no separate object beyond the perceptible magnitudes classify the forms that are objects of thought with those that are [*116*] objects of perception, and that [for them] the things spoken of by abstraction, and all states and affections of objects of perception, are of this sort, <but while the [abstract objects] are more detached from matter>,[228] and the [perceptible qualities] as it were confounded with it, all [on this view] nonetheless depend on it. This is indicated by the fact that a person blind and deaf from birth could not learn geometry, and perhaps not even form an image of a circle or a triangle, except maybe one that was hot, cold, sweet, bitter, or with a pleasant or foul odour,[229] [all qualities] that he also perceives. And from the outset the intellect collects [the concepts of] one, two, or number from the objects of perception. That is why even now[230] when it thinks about such things, it must do so along with an image, for images are like sensations, except that they are without matter.

116.10 (432a10-12): Things that are spoken of and thought in combination are clearly different from images. For while the same images of day and light remain in the soul, the intellect combines them in various ways in the [statements] "If it is day, it is light," or "It is day and it is light," or "It is day but it is not light," or "Let there be day and let there be light." And all these combinations are different both from one another and from the [corresponding] images, and truth and falsity exist with respect to the combination, but they are not in the images.

---

[228] The supplement followed is: <*alla ta men aphestêkota mallon tês hulês*>. See Heinze's apparatus criticus *ad* 116.2. Omitted is *hôsper* before *aphestêkota* which, unlike the following *sumpephurmena* (cf. note 196), is not metaphorical.

[229] Omitted is Heinze's supplement *hôs* at 116.5; the translated text follows De Falco (who follows Torraca) in omitting the definite articles before *euôdes* and *dusôdes* at 116.6.

[230] That is, in its mature state. The account of the evolution of the intellect at 95.9-32 is presupposed here.

116.17 (432a12-14): How will the uncombined and primary thoughts differ from being images? Well, not even these[231] [thoughts] are images, but they are not without images. The thought derived from Socrates and the image [of him] are not, that is, identical; instead images are a kind of imprint and trace[232] of perception, and like an affection[233] (if I could have you think of affection as often spoken of before),[234] whereas the thought is the activity of the intellect towards the underlying[235] image. The intellect, you see, uses the image in this and [other] elaborate ways by making changes both in the inflections [of nouns] and in the definite articles.[236]

---

[231] Retained is *tauta* (116.18) from the manuscripts of Themistius; Heinze altered it to *talla*, the reading in nearly all the manuscripts of Aristotle at 432a13.

[232] Cf. Alexander *De Anima* 72.11-13 where *tupos* ("imprint") is said to be a metaphorical term for the trace (*ichnos*) left by sense perception.

[233] *hôsper peisis* (116.20); *peisis* has essentially the same meaning as *pathos*, the term usually rendered "affection."

[234] Cf. Themistius' discussion at 92.19-23 (on *De Anima* 3.3) where he warns against the danger of applying the metaphor of imprinting literally in characterizing perception or the imagination. Cf. Todd (1981) 51-52 with notes 27, 32, 33 for the wider context.

[235] *hupokeimenon* (116.22). Cf. 100.30 above where the imagination is described as "matter for the potential intellect," and the similar use of *hupokeimenon* in that context at 100.33 and 100.37.

[236] Themistius might have been expected to refer to the logical connectives identified in the statements listed at 116.12-14 above. He chooses instead to envisage manipulations of thoughts for which the linguistic correlate is a noun, without indicating the effect of these changes on the structure of the statements in which the noun occurs. Certainly *arthron* (116.23), here at least, cannot carry the meaning "connective"; it must refer to the articles that accompany inflected nouns.

Glossary

abstraction	*aphairesis*
accidentally	*kata sumbebêkos*
be active	*energein*
activity, actuality	*energeia*
active, actual, in actuality	*energeiâi* (dative case), *kat'energeian*
adaptability, natural	*euphuia*
be affected	*paschein*
affection	*pathos*
apprehension	*antilêpsis*
apprehend	*antilambanesthai*
apprehending, capable of	*antilêptikos*
become, come into existence	*ginesthai*
combine	*suntithenai, sumplekein*
combination	*sunthesis, sumplokê*
complete (adj.)	*teleios*
complete, bring to completion	*teleioun*
completion	*teleiotês, teleiôsis*
compound, compounded	*sunthetos, sunkeimenos*
craft	*technê*
desire	*orexis*
discern (*De Intellectu*)	*krinein*
discerning, capable of (*De Intellectu*)	*kritikos*
divided	*diairetos*
emotion	*thumos*
essence	*ousia, to ti ên einai*

estimable	*timios*
existing things	*ta onta*
faculty	*dunamis*
final state	*telos*
form	*eidos, morphê*
forms, enmattered	*ta enula* (*eidê*)*
forms, immaterial	*ta aula* (*eidê*)*
from without	*exôthen, thurathen*
grasp	*katalambanein*
image	*phantasma*
imagination	*phantasia*
immortal	*athanatos*
imperishable	*aphthartos*
indivisible/undivided	*adiairetos*
intellect	*nous*
intellect, active	*ho energeiâi* (dative case) (*nous*)*
intellect, common	*ho koinos* (*nous*)*
intellect, divine	*ho theios* (*nous*)*
intellect, enmattered	*ho enulos* (*nous*)
intellect, from without	*ho exôthen/ thurathen* (*nous*)*
intellect, immortal	*ho athanatos* (*nous*)
intellect, material	*ho hulikos* (*nous*)*
intellect, passive	*ho pathêtikos* (*nous*)*
intellect, potential	*ho dunamei* (*nous*)*
intellect, productive	*ho poiêtikos* (*nous*)*
intellect, theoretical	*ho theorêtikos* (*nous*)*
judge, make judgments	*krinein*
knowledge	*epistêmê*
knowledge, body of	*epistêmê*

* indicates that the nouns *nous* and *eidê* are often omitted in these Greek phrases, though they are almost always supplied in the English translation.

matter	*hulê*
move	*kinein*
movement	*kinêsis*
nature, by nature	*phusis, phusei*
objects, abstract	*ta ex aphaireseôs*
object of thought	*noêton*
object of perception	*aisthêton*
passion (sc. of the soul)	*pathos*
perception	*aisthêsis*
perceive	*aisthanesthai*
perishable	*phthartos*
potential, potentially, in potentiality	*dunamei*
potentiality, power	*dunamis*
privation	*sterêsis*
reason (noun)	*logos* (Themistius 93.33)
reasoning	*theoria*
reasoning, discursive	*dianoeisthai*
receive	*dechesthai*
receiving, capable of	*dektikos*
sensation	*aisthêma*
separate	*chorizein*
shape (cf. form)	*morphê*
simple	*haplous*
soul	*psuchê*
state (of possession/possessing)	*hexis*
state, positive	*hexis* (= Aristotle *De Anima* 430a15)
substance	*ousia*
substrate	*hupokeimenon*
think	*noein*
think about	*theorein*
thinking	*noêsis*
thought	*noêma*

unaffected	*apathês*
uncombined	*haplous*
uncompounded	*asunthetos*
undivided	*diairetos*
universal	*katholou*
wishing	*boulêsis*

BIBLIOGRAPHY

A. EDITIONS OF PRINCIPAL GREEK TEXTS CITED
(* denotes text used in the translations)

Aristotle

Aristotle: De Anima. Ed. R.D. Hicks. Cambridge: 1907; repr., Amsterdam: 1965.

Aristotelis De Anima. Ed. W.D. Ross. Oxford Classical Texts. Oxford: 1956.

Aristotle: De Anima. Ed. with comm. Sir David Ross. Oxford: 1961.

Aristotelis Tractatus De Anima. Ed. P. Siwek. Rome: 1965.

Alexander of Aphrodisias

De Anima Liber cum Mantissa. Ed. I. Bruns, SA 2.1. Berlin: 1887).

*De Intellectu = SA 2.1: 106.18-113.24. For the Arabic version see Finnegan (1956a); for the medieval Latin version see Théry 74-82. French translations are available in Moraux (1942) 185-194, and Carrière *et al.* 19-37; an English translation can be found in Fotinis 137-153.

Quaestiones: De Fato: De Mixtione. Ed. I. Bruns. SA 2.2. Berlin: 1892.

Alexandre d'Aphrodise: Traité du destin. Ed. and trans. P. Thillet. Paris: 1984.

Themistius

Themistiou Paraphrasis tôn Peri Psuchês Aristotelous. Ed. L. Spengel, *Themistii Paraphrases Aristotelis librorum quae supersunt.* Leipzig: 1866. 2: 1-231.

*In Libros Aristotelis De Anima Paraphrasis (= *In De Anima*). Ed. R. Heinze, CAG 5.3. Berlin: 1899. For the Arabic version

see Lyons (1973); for the medieval Latin version see Verbeke (1957); for an Italian translation see De Falco. *Analyticorum Posteriorum Paraphrasis* (= *In Analytica Posteriora*). Ed. M. Wallies, CAG 5.1. Berlin: 1900. *In Aristotelis Metaphysicorum Librum Λ Paraphrasis: Hebraice et Latine* (= *In Metaphysica Lambda*). Ed. S. Landauer, CAG 5.5. Berlin: 1903. For an edition of the remains of the Arabic version see Badawi (1947).

B. Translations, Secondary Works and Other Editions

Accattino, P. "Alessandro di Afrodisia e Aristotele di Mitilene." *Elenchos* 6 (1985): 67-74.

Allan, D.J. *The Philosophy of Aristotle.* 2nd. ed. Oxford: 1970.

Armstrong, A.H. "The Background of the Doctrine 'That the intelligibles are not outside the intellect'." In *Les Sources de Plotin,* pp. 391-413. Entretiens Hardt 5. Vandœuvres and Geneva: 1960. Reprinted in A. Hilary Armstrong, *Plotinian and Christian Studies,* ch. 4. London: 1979.

Atkinson, Michael *Plotinus: Ennead V.1: On the Three Principal Hypostases: A Commentary.* Oxford: 1983.

Badawi, A. (1947) *Aristū 'inda'l-'Arab.* Cairo: 1947.

Badawi, A. (1968) *La transmission de la philosophie grecque au monde arabe.* Paris: 1968.

Ballériaux, O. *D'Aristote à Thémistius: Contribution à une histoire de la noétique d'après Aristote.* Dissertation, Liège: 1943.

Barbotin, E. *La Théorie Aristotélicienne de l'intellect d'après Théophraste.* Louvain and Paris: 1954.

Bastait's, M. Review of Todd (1976), *Scriptorium* 33 (1979): 133-134.

Bazán, Bernardo C. (1973) "L'authenticité du 'De intellectu' attribué à Alexandre d'Aphrodise." *Revue Philosophique de Louvain* 71 (1973): 468-487.

Bazán, Bernardo C. (1976-77) "La noética di Temistio (c.

320-390)." *Revista Venezolana de Filosofia* 5-6 (1976-77): 51-82.

Becchi, F. "Aspasio e i peripatetici posteriori: la formula definitiva della passione." *Prometheus* 9 (1983): 83-104.

Berti, E. "The Intellection of Indivisibles According to Aristotle, *De Anima* III.6." In *Aristotle on Mind and the Senses* Proceedings of the Seventh Symposium Aristotelicum, ed. G.E.R. Lloyd and G.E.L. Owen, pp. 141-164. Cambridge: 1978.

Blumenthal, H.J. (1968) "Plotinus *Ennead* IV.3.20-21 and Its Sources." *Archiv für Geschichte der Philosophie* 50 (1968): 254-261.

Blumenthal, H.J. (1971) *Plotinus' Psychology: His Doctrines of the Embodied Soul.* The Hague: 1971.

Blumenthal, H.J. (1979a) "Photius on Themistius (Cod. 74): Did Themistius Write Commentaries on Aristotle?" *Hermes* 107 (1979): 168-182.

Blumenthal, H.J. (1979b) "Themistius: The Last Peripatetic Commentator on Aristotle?" In *Arktouros: Hellenic Studies presented to Bernard M. Knox,* ed. G. Bowersock *et al.,* pp. 391-400. Berlin and New York: 1979.

Brown, H.V.P. "Avicenna and the Christian Philosophers in Baghdad." In *Islamic Philosophy and the Classical Tradition: Studies presented to R. Walzer,* ed. S. Stern *et al.,* pp. 35-48. Oxford: 1972.

Browne, G.M. "Ad Themistium Arabum." *Illinois Classical Studies* 11 (1986): 223-245.

Carrière, B. *et al. Le PERI NOU attribué à Alexandre d'Aphrodise,* with introduction, translation and notes. Dissertation, Montreal: 1961.

Cornford, F.M. *Plato's Cosmology: The "Timaeus" of Plato,* trans., with a running commentary. London: 1937.

De Corte, M. *La doctrine de l'intelligence chez Aristote.* Paris: 1934.

Cranz, F. Edward (1961) "Alexander Aphrodisiensis." In *Catalogus Translationum et Commentariorum: Mediaeval and*

Renaissance Latin Translations and Commentaries, ed. Paul Oskar Kristeller, 1:77-135. Washington: 1961.

Cranz, F. Edward (1971) "Alexander Aphrodisiensis: Addenda et Corrigenda." In *Catalogus Translationum et Commentariorum: Mediaeval and Renaissance Latin Translations and Commentaries.* Ed. Paul Oskar Kristeller, 2:411-422. Washington: 1971.

Dagron, Gilbert "L'Empire romain d'Orient du IVe siècle et les traditions politiques d'hellenisme: le témoinage de Thémistios." *Travaux et Mémoires* [Centre de recherche d'histoire et civilisation byzantines] 3 (1967): 1-242.

Davidson, H.A. "Alfarabi and Avicenna on the Active Intellect." *Viator* 3 (1972): 109-178.

Donini, P. (1970) "L'anima e gli elementi nel *de anima* di Alessandro di Afrodisia." *Atti dell'Accademia delle Scienze di Torino* (Classe di Scienze Morali, Storiche e Filologiche) 105 (1970-1971): 61-107.

Donini, P. (1974) *Tre Studi sull'Aristotelismo nel II secolo D.C..* Historica, Politica, Philosophica 7. Turin: 1974.

Donini, P. (1982) *Le scuole, L'anima, L'impero: la filosofia antica da Antioco a Plotino.* Turin: 1982.

Faggin, G. "Temistio." *Enciclopedia Filosofica.* 2nd. ed., 4: 370-371. Venice and Rome: 1957.

De Falco, V. *Parafrasi dei libri di Aristotele sull'anima,* trans. V. De Falco. Padua: 1965.

Finnegan, J. (1956a) ed. "Texte arabe du PERI NOU d'Alexandre d'Aphrodise." *Mélanges de l'Université Saint Joseph* 33.2: 157-202. Beirut: 1956.

Finnegan, J. (1956b) "Avicenna's Refutation of Porphyrius." In *Avicenna Commemoration Volume,* ed. V. Courtois, pp. 187-203. Calcutta: 1956.

Finnegan, J. (1957) "Al-Fārābī et le PERI NOU d'Alexandre d' Aphrodise." In *Mélanges Louis Massignon,* 2:133-152. 3 vols. Damascus: 1956-1957.

Fotinis, A.P. *The De Anima of Alexander of Aphrodisias: A Translation and Commentary.* Washington: 1979.

Genequand, C. *Ibn Rushd's Metaphysics: A Translation with Introduction of Ibn Rushd's Commentary on Aristotle's Metaphysics Book Lam.* Leiden: 1984.

Gilson, E. "Les sources gréco-arabes de l'augustinisme avicennisant." *Archives d'histoire doctrinale et litteraire du moyen âge* 4 (1929): 5-149.

Gottschalk, H.B. (1985) Review of Moraux (1984), *Liverpool Classical Monthly* 10.8 (1985): 122-128.

Gottschalk, H.B. (1987) "Aristotelian Philosophy in the Roman World from the Time of Cicero to the End of the Second Century AD." *Aufstieg und Niedergang der römischen Welt* 2.36.2 (1987): 1079-1174.

Goulet, R. "L'oracle d'Apollon dans la *Vie de Plotin*." In L. Brisson *et al, Porphyre, La Vie de Plotin: Travaux Préliminaires*, pp. 371-412. Histoire des doctrines de l'antiquité classique 6. Paris: 1982.

Grabmann, M. (1929) "Mittelalterliche lateinische Übersetzungen von Schriften der Aristoteles-Kommentatoren Johannes Philoponos, Alexander von Aphrodisias und Themistios." *Sitzungsberichte der bayerischen Akademie der Wissenschaften*, Phil.-Hist. Abt. [Munich: 1929]: Hft. 7. Reprinted in Martin Grabmann, *Gesammelte Akademieabhandlungen*, 1: 497-564. 3 vols. Paderborn, Munich, Vienna, Zurich: 1979.

Grabmann, M. (1936) "Mittelalterliche Deutung und Umbildung der aristotelischen Lehre vom NOUS POIETIKOS." *Sitzungsberichte der Bayerischen Akademie der Wissenschaften*, Phil.-Hist. Abt. [Munich: 1936]: Hft. 4. Reprinted in Martin Grabmann, *Gesammelte Akademieabhandlungen*, 1: 1021-1122. 3 vols. Paderborn, Munich, Vienna, Zurich: 1979.

Günsz, A. *Die Abhandlung Alexanders von Aphrodisias über den Intellekt.* Dissertation, Berlin: 1887.

Hager, F.P. "Die Aristotelesinterpretation des Alexanders von Aphrodisias und die Aristoteleskritik Plotins bezüglich der Lehre von Geist." *Archiv für Geschichte der Philosophie* 46 (1964): 174-187.

Hamelin, O. *La théorie de l'intellect d'après Aristote et ses commentateurs.* Paris: 1953.

Hamlyn, D. *Aristotle's De Anima: Books II and III*, trans. D.W. Hamlyn. Oxford: 1968.

Hartmann, E. *Substance, Body, and Soul: Aristotelian Investigations.* Princeton: 1977.

Heiland, H. *Aristoclis Messenii Reliquiae.* Dissertation, Giessen: 1925.

Henry, P. "Une comparaison chez Aristote, Alexandre et Plotin." In *Les Sources de Plotin*, pp. 429-449. Entretiens Hardt 5. Vandœuvres and Geneva: 1960.

Himmereich, W. *Eudaimonia: Die Lehre des Plotin von der Selbstverwirklichung des Menschen.* Forschungen zur neueren Philosophie und ihrer Geschichte, n.f. 13. Würzburg: 1959.

Huby, Pamela M. "Medieval Evidence for Theophrastus' Discussion of the Intellect." In *Theophrastus of Eresus: On His Life and Work*, ed. William W. Fortenbaugh *et al.* pp. 165-181. Rutgers University Studies in Classical Humanities 2. New Brunswick and Oxford: 1985.

Hyman, A. "Aristotle's Theory of the Intellect and its Interpretation by Averroes." In *Studies in Aristotle*, ed. D.J. O'Meara, pp. 161-191. Studies in Philosophy and the History of Philosophy 9. Washington: 1981.

Jones, A.H.M. *et al. The Prosopography of the Later Roman Empire*, vol 1: *A.D. 260-395.* Cambridge: 1971.

Kahn, C.H. "The Role of NOUS in the Cognition of First Principles in *Posterior Analytics* II.19." In *Aristotle on Science: The Posterior Analytics*, (Proceedings of the Eighth Symposium Aristotelicum), ed. E. Berti, pp. 385-414. Padua: 1981.

Kurfess, H. *Zur Geschichte der Erklärung der aristotelischen Lehre vom sogennanten NOUS POETIKOS und PATHETIKOS.* Tübingen: 1911.

Lloyd, A.C. (1976) "The Principle that the Cause is Greater than Its Effect." *Phronesis* 21 (1976): 146-156.

Lloyd, A.C. (1986) "Non-propositional Thought in Plotinus." *Phronesis* 31 (1986): 258-265

Lohr, C. ed. *Commentaria in Aristotelem Graeca: Versiones Latinae XVII, Themistii paraphraseos.* Frankfurt: 1978.

Lowe, M.F. "Aristotle on Kinds of Thinking." *Phronesis* 28 (1983): 17-30.

Lynch, J.P. *Aristotle's School: A Study of a Greek Educational Institution.* Berkeley and Los Angeles: 1972.

Lyons, M.C. (1955) "An Arabic Translation of the Commentary of Themistius." *Bulletin of the School of Oriental and African Studies* 17 (1955): 426-435.

Lyons, M.C. (1973) *An Arabic Translation of Themistius' Commentary on Aristotle's De Anima,* ed. M.C. Lyons. London: 1973.

Mahoney, E.P. (1969) "Nicoletto Vernia and Agostino Nifo on Alexander of Aphrodisias: An Unnoticed Dispute." *Rivista critica di storia della filosofia* 23 (1969): 269-296.

Mahoney, E.P. (1973) "Themistius and the Agent Intellect in James of Viterbo and Other Thirteenth-Century Philosophers (Saint Thomas, Siger of Brabant and Henry Bate)." *Augustiniana* 23 (1973): 422-467.

Mahoney, E.P. (1982a) "Neoplatonism, the Greek Commentators, and Renaissance Aristotelianism." In *Neoplatonism and Christian Thought,* ed. D.J. O'Meara, pp. 169-177. Albany: 1982.

Mahoney, E.P. (1982b) "Sense, Intellect, and Imagination in Albert, Thomas, and Siger." In *The Cambridge History of Later Medieval Philosophy,* ed. Norman Kretzman, Anthony Kenny, Jan Pinborg, pp. 602-622. Cambridge: 1982.

Mansion, A. "L'immortalité de l'âme et d'intellect d'après Aristote." *Revue Philosophique de Louvain* 51 (1953): 444-472.

Martin, S.B. "The Nature of the Human Intellect as It is Expounded in Themistius' 'Paraphrasis in Libros Aristotelis de anima'." In *The Quest for the Absolute,* ed. F.J. Adelman, pp. 1-21. Boston College Studies in Philosophy 1. Boston: 1966.

Martin, Th. "Questions connexes sur deux Sosigènes." *Annales de la Faculté des Lettres de Bordeaux* 1 (1879): 174-187.

Martorana, A.L. "Il maestro di Alessandro di Afrodisia." *Sophia* 36 (1968): 365-367.

McDowell, J. *Plato: Theaetetus*, trans. with notes. Clarendon Plato Series. Oxford: 1973.

Massignon, L. "Notes sur le texte original arabe du 'De Intellectu' d'Al Fārābī." *Archives d'histoire doctrinale et littéraire du môyen âge* 4 (1929): 151-158.

Merlan, P. (1963) *Monopsychism, Mysticism, Metaconsciousness: Problems of the Soul in the Neoaristotelian and Neoplatonic Tradition.* The Hague: 1963.

Merlan,P. (1967) "Greek Philosophy from Plato to Plotinus." In *The Cambridge History of Later Greek and Early Medieval Philosophy*, ed. A.H. Armstrong, pp. 11-132. Cambridge: 1967.

Merlan, P. (1970) "Alexander of Aphrodisias." In *Dictionary of Scientific Biography*, 1:117-120. New York: 1970.

Montanari, E. Review of Todd (1976), *Annali della Scuola Normale Superiore di Pisa* (Classe di Lettere e Filosofia), ser. III 10.4 (1980): 1438-1448.

Moraux, P. (1942) *Alexandre d'Aphrodise: Exégète de la noétique d'Aristote.* Bibliothèque de la faculté de philosophie et lettres de l'Université de Liège 99. Liège and Paris: 1942.

Moraux, P. (1955) "À propos du *nous thurathen* chez Aristote." In *Autour d'Aristote: Receuil d'études de philosophie ancienne et medievale offert à Monseigneur A. Mansion*, pp. 255-295. Louvain: 1955.

Moraux, P. (1967) "Aristoteles, der Lehrer Alexanders von Aphrodisias." *Archiv für Geschichte der Philosophie* 49 (1967): 169-182.

Moraux, P. (1973) *Der Aristotelismus bei den Griechen.* Vol. 1. Berlin: 1973.

Moraux, P. (1978a) "Le *De Anima* dans la tradition grecque: Quelques aspects de l'interpretation du traité, de Théophraste à Thémistius." In *Aristotle on Mind and the Senses* (Proceedings of the Seventh Symposium Aristotelicum), ed. G.E.R. Lloyd and G.E.L. Owen, pp. 281-324. Cambridge: 1978.

Moraux, P. (1978b) Review of Donini (1974), *Gnomon* 50 (1978): 532-536.

Moraux, P. (1981) Review of Todd (1976), *Gnomon* 53 (1981): 641-646.

Moraux, P. (1984) *Der Aristotelismus bei den Griechen.* Vol. 2. Berlin: 1984.

Moraux, P. (1985) "Ein neues Zeugnis über Aristoteles, den Lehrer Alexanders von Aphrodisias." *Archiv für Geschichte der Philosophie* 67 (1985): 266-269.

Movia, G. (1970a) *Alessandro di Afrodisia tra naturalismo e misticismo.* Padua: 1970.

Movia, G. (1970b) "Alessandro di Afrodisia: Naturalista o Mistico?" In *Saggi e ricerche su Alessandro di Afrodisia, Avicenna, Miceli, Brentano, Jaspers, Ingarden, Carr, Storiografica filosofica italiana, Ebraismo,* ed. C. Giacon, pp. 15-23. Pubblicazioni dell'Istituto di Storia della filosophia e del Centro per richerche di filosofia medioevale, n.s. 9. Padua: 1970.

Nardi, B. *S. Tomasso d'Aquino: Trattato sull'unità dell'intelletto contro gli Averroisti,* trans. B. Nardi. Florence: 1947.

Norman, R. "Aristotle's Philosopher-God." *Phronesis* 14 (1969): 63-74. Reprinted in *Articles on Aristotle,* ed. J. Barnes *et al.,* 4:93-102. 4 vols. London and New York: 1975-1979.

Nutton, V. "Galen in the Eyes of his Contemporaries." *Bulletin of the history of medicine* 58 (1984): 315-324.

Owens, J. "A Note on Aristotle, *De Anima* 3.4, 429b9." *Phoenix* 30 (1976): 107-118. Reprinted in *Aristotle: The Collected Papers of Joseph Owens,* ed. J.R. Catan, pp. 99-108. Albany: 1981.

Pépin, J. "Héraclès et son reflet dans le néoplatonisme." In *Le Néoplatonisme,* pp. 167-192. Colloques internationaux du Centre National de la Recherche Scientifique, Royaumont, 1969. Paris: 1971.

Peters, F.E. (1968a) *Aristoteles Arabus: The Oriental Translations and Commentaries on the Aristotelian Corpus.* Leiden: 1968.

Peters, F.E. (1968b) *Aristotle and the Arabs: The Aristotelian Tradition in Islam.* New York and London: 1968.

Pines, S. (1961) "Omne quod movetur necesse est ab aliquo moveri: A Refutation of Galen by Alexander of Aphrodisias and the Theory of Motion." *Isis* 52 (1961): 21-54.

Pines, S. (1987) "Some Distinctive Metaphysical Conceptions in Themistius' Commentary on Book Lambda and Their Place in the History of Philosophy." In *Aristoteles: Werk und Wirkung: Paul Moraux gewidmet,* ed. J. Wiesner, 2: 177-204. 2 vols. Berlin and New York: 1985-1987.

Preus, A. Review of Fotinis, *Journal of the History of Philosophy* 20 (1982): 427-429.

Randall, J.H. *The School of Padua and the Emergence of Modern Science.* Istituto filosofico Columbiana-Padovano, Saggi e Testi 1. Padua: 1961.

Rist, J.M. (1962) "The Indefinite Dyad and Intelligible Matter in Plotinus." *Classical Quarterly* n.s. 12 (1962): 99-107.

Rist, J.M. (1966a) "On Tracking Alexander of Aphrodisias." *Archiv für Geschichte der Philosophie* 48 (1966): 82-90.

Rist, J.M. (1966b) "Notes on Aristotle *De Anima* 3.5." *Classical Philology* 61 (1966): 8-20. Reprinted in *Essays in Ancient Greek Philosophy,* ed. J. Anton and G. Kustas, pp. 505-512. Albany: 1971.

Robert, L. "Inscriptions d'Aphrodisias." *L'Antiquité Classique* 35 (1966): 397-432.

Rose, V. *Aristotelis Fragmenta.* 3rd. ed. Leipzig: 1886.

Schroeder, F.M. (1981) "The Analogy of the Active Intellect to Light in the 'De Anima' of Alexander of Aphrodisias." *Hermes* 109 (1981): 215-225.

Schroeder, F.M. (1982) "The Potential or Material Intellect and the Authorship of the *De Intellectu:* A Reply to B.C. Bazán." *Symbolae Osloenses* 57 (1982): 115-125.

Schroeder, F.M. (1984) "Light and the Active Intellect in Alexander and Plotinus." *Hermes* 112 (1984): 239-248.

Schroeder, F.M. (1986) "Conversion and Consciousness in Plotinus." *Hermes* 114 (1986): 186-195.

Schroeder, F.M. (1987) "Ammonius Saccas." *Aufstieg und Niedergang der römischen Welt* 2.36.1 (1987): 493-526.

Schwyzer, H.-R. "Plotin." In Pauly-Wissowa, *Real-Encyclopädie* 21.1 (1951): cols. 471-592.

Sharples, R.W. (1975) "Responsibility, Chance, and Not-Being (Alexander of Aphrodisias, *Mantissa* 169-172)." *Bulletin of the Institute of Classical Studies* 22 (1975): 37-64.

Sharples, R.W. (1983) *Alexander of Aphrodisias on Fate*. London: 1983.

Sharples, R.W. (1986) Review of Thillet (1984), *Classical Review* n.s. 36 (1986): 33-35.

Sharples, R.W. (1987) "Alexander of Aphrodisias: Scholasticism and Innovation." *Aufstieg und Niedergang der römischen Welt* 2.36.2 (1987): 1176-1243.

Sorabji, R. *Time, Creation and the Continuum: Theories in Antiquity and the Early Middle Ages*. London: 1983.

Sprague, R.K. "A Parallel with *De Anima* III.5." *Phronesis* 17 (1972): 250-251.

Stabile, K. *The Origins of the Problem of the Medieval Noetic: Aristotle or Alexander of Aphrodisias?* Dissertation, Fordham University: 1974.

Steel, C. "Des commentaires d'Aristote par Thémistius?" *Revue Philosophique de Louvain* 71 (1973): 669-680.

Stump, E. *Boethius's "De topicis differentiis,"* trans. with notes and essays. Ithaca and London: 1978.

Van Steenberghen, F. (1955) *The Philosophical Movement in the Thirteenth Century*. Edinburgh: 1955.

Van Steenberghen, F. (1970) *Aristotle in the West: The Origins of Latin Aristotelianism*. New York: 1970.

Stegemann, W. "Themistios." In Pauly Wissowa, *Real-Encyclopädie*, Zw. Rh. 5 (1934): cols. 1642-1680.

Szlezák, T. *Platon und Aristoteles in der Nuslehre Plotins*. Basel and Stuttgart: 1979.

Théry, G. *Autour du décret de 1210, II: Alexandre d'Aphrodise: Aperçu sur l'influence de sa noétique*. Le Saulchoir Kain: 1926.

Thillet, P. (1981) "Matérialisme et théorie de l'âme et de l'intellect chez Alexandre d'Aphrodise." *Revue Philosophique* 171 (1981): 5-24.

Thillet, P. (1984) ed. and trans. *Alexandre d'Aphrodise: Traité du destin*. Paris: 1984.

Todd, R.B. (1972) "Alexander of Aphrodisias and the Alexandrian *Quaestiones* II.12." *Philologus* 116 (1972): 293-305.

Todd, R.B. (1973) "The Stoic Common Notions: A Reexamination and Reinterpretation." *Symbolae Osloenses* 48 (1973): 47-75.

Todd, R.B. (1974) "Lexicographical Notes on Alexander of Aphrodisias' Philosophical Terminology." *Glotta* 52 (1974): 207-215.

Todd, R.B. (1976) *Alexander of Aphrodisias on Stoic Physics*. Leiden: 1976.

Todd, R.B. (1977) "Galenic Medical Ideas in the Greek Aristotelian Commentators." *Symbolae Osloenses* 52 (1977): 117-134.

Todd, R.B. (1981) "Themistius and the Traditional Interpretation of Aristotle's Theory of *Phantasia*." *Acta Classica* 24 (1981): 49-59.

Trabucco, F. "Il problema di 'de philosophia' di Aristocle di Messene et la sua dottrina." *Acme* 11 (1958): 97-150.

Überweg, F. *Grundriss der Geschichte der Philosophie*. Bd. I. 13th. ed., rev. K. Prächter, Tübingen: 1953.

Verbeke, G. (1957) ed. *Thémistius: Commentaire sur le traité de l'âme d'Aristote, traduction de Guillaume de Moerbeke*. Corpus Latinum Commentariorum in Aristotelem Graecorum 1. Louvain and Paris: 1957.

Verbeke, G. (1966), ed. *Jean Philopon: Commentaire sur le De Anima d'Aristotle, traduction de Guillaume de Moerbeke*. Corpus Latinum Commentariorum in Aristotelem Graecorum 3. Louvain and Paris: 1966.

Verbeke, G. (1976) "Themistius." In *Dictionary of Scientific Biography*, 13: 307-309. New York: 1976.

Wilpert, P. "Die Ausgestaltung der aristotelischen Lehre vom

Intellectus agens bei griechischen Kommentatoren und in der Scholastik des 13. Jahrhunderts." *Beiträge zur Geschichte der Philosophie und Theologie des Mittelalters,* Supplbd. 3.1 (1935): 447-462.

Zeller, E. *Die Philosophie der Griechen in ihrer geschichtlichen Entwicklung dargestellt.* Vol. 3.1. 5th. ed., rev. W. Nestle, Leipzig: 1923.

Zorzetti, N. Review of Donini (1970), *Studi Medievali* 12 (1971): 263-268.

Index Locorum

General Index

DATE